hamlyn
QuickCook

W9-AGE-796

hamlyn
QuickCook
Family Meals

Recipes by Emma Jane Frost

Every dish, three ways—you choose!
30 minutes | 20 minutes | 10 minutes

An Hachette UK company
www.hachette.co.uk

First published in Great Britain in 2012 by Hamlyn,
a division of Octopus Publishing Group Ltd
Endeavour House, 189 Shaftesbury Avenue, London WC2H 8JY
www.octopusbooks.co.uk

Distributed in the US by Hachette Book Group USA
237 Park Avenue, New York, NY 10017 USA
www.octopusbooksusa.com

Distributed in Canada by Canadian Manda Group
165 Dufferin Street, Toronto, Ontario, Canada M6K 3H6

Recipes by Emma Jane Frost
Copyright © Octopus Publishing Group Ltd 2012

ISBN: 978-0-60062-402-8

Printed and bound in China

1 2 3 4 5 6 7 8 9 10

Standard level spoon measurements are used in all recipes

Ovens should be preheated to the specified temperature. If using a fan-assisted
oven, follow the manufacturer's instructions for adjusting the time and temperature.

Eggs should be medium unless otherwise stated. The FDA advises that eggs should
not be consumed raw. This book contains some dishes made with raw or lightly
cooked eggs. It is prudent for more vulnerable people, such as pregnant and nursing
mothers, invalids, the elderly, babies, and young children, to avoid uncooked or lightly
cooked dishes made with eggs.

This book includes dishes made with nuts and nut derivatives. It is advisable for those
with known allergic reactions to nuts and nut derivatives and those who may be
potentially vulnerable to these allergies, such as pregnant and nursing mothers,
invalids, the elderly, babies, and children, to avoid dishes made with nuts and nut oils.
It is also prudent to check the labels of prepared ingredients for the possible inclusion
of nut derivatives.

Contents

Introduction

30 20 10—quick, quicker, quickest

This book offers a new and flexible approach to meal-planning for busy cooks and lets you choose the recipe option that best fits the time you have available. Inside you will find 360 dishes that will inspire you and motivate you to get cooking every day of the year. All the recipes take a maximum of 30 minutes to cook. Some take as little as 20 minutes and, amazingly, many take only 10 minutes. With a bit of preparation, you can easily try out one new recipe from this book each night and slowly you will build a wide and exciting portfolio of recipes to suit your needs.

How Does It Work?

Every recipe in the QuickCook series can be cooked one of three ways—a 30-minute version, a 20-minute version, or a super-quick and easy 10-minute version. At the beginning of each chapter you'll find recipes listed by time. Choose a dish based on how much time you have and turn to that page.

You'll find the main recipe in the middle of the page with a beautiful photograph and two time-variations below.

If you enjoy the dish, you can go back and cook the other time options. If you liked the 30-minute Smoky Chicken and Shrimp Paella, but only have 10 minutes to spare, then you'll find a way to cook it using cheat ingredients or clever shortcuts.

If you love the ingredients and flavors of the 10-minute Mango and Spinach Salad with Warm Peanut Chicken, why not try something more substantial like the 20-minute Chicken and Mango Kebabs, or be inspired to cook a more elaborate version like a Chicken Stir-Fry with Mango and Peanut Sauce. Alternatively, browse through all of the 360 delicious recipes, find something that takes your eye—then cook the version that fits your time frame.

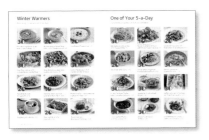

Or, for easy inspiration, turn to the gallery on pages 12–19 to get an instant overview by themes, such as Winter Warmers or Weekend Treats.

QuickCook online

To make life even easier, you can use the special code on each recipe page to email yourself a recipe card for printing, or email a text-only shopping list to your phone. Go to www.hamlynquickcook.com and enter the recipe code at the bottom of each page.

FAM-MEAT-GES

QuickCook Family Meals

In today's modern society, there is a great amount of pressure on a family's time. Parents tend to work, children have more and more extracurricular activities, and generally, life is packed to the gills with activity and busyness. It is not a surprise then that supermarket ready-meals have risen so dramatically in popularity over the last decade. How many times have we got home at the end of a busy day to find ourselves looking into an uninspiring refrigerator and wondering what on earth we are going to feed everyone? It is too easy to pop a cheap ready-meal into the microwave or call for an expensive, fat-filled take out. But our message to you in this book is that you can cook a really tasty, fabulous-looking family supper with limited ingredients, quickly and easily.

You've heard it said about DIY, but it is also true of cookery. Fail to prepare and you prepare to fail! Whether you are an experienced cook or a complete novice, if you don't have a quick think in the morning before work about what meal you're going to be rustling up for your family that evening, come 6 o'clock you'll be spending unnecessary amounts of time defrosting food and nipping to the corner store for missing ingredients. Much as it sounds obvious, do take a few minutes to plan in the morning, and get fish or meat out of the freezer ready, and make a quick shopping list so you can get whatever you need when you're out that day.

The Art of Multitasking

The best chefs in the world are the ones who can be cooking 20 things at once while keeping calm and in control! We are not asking you to cook 20 things at once, but we do suggest you learn the great art of multitasking in the kitchen. For instance, our Apricot-Glazed Ham Steaks with Paprika Potatoes on page 92 require you to put the potatoes on to boil at the beginning, then while they are cooking, to start pan-cooking the other ingredients. While you are making the sauce, you have to go back to finish off the potatoes and then the whole meal comes together at roughly the same time. Without a bit of juggling with your burner, broiler and oven, it will be impossible to muster up a meal in 30 minutes or less, but follow our recipes in the order they say and you'll be pleasantly surprised at how quickly supper comes together.

The Right Tools for the Job

With the right ingredients in stock, the art of multitasking mastered, and motivation levels high, the only thing left to consider are the tools at hand. Do not underestimate how vitally important good tools are to help make the cooking process not just easier but a lot more enjoyable. The first and most important tool is a large, heavy skillet. Without one of these many of our recipes will be tricky to master. A thick, heavy base to your pan gives a more even temperature spread and can therefore prevent burning.

Knives are also vital to get right. A knife that is regularly sharpened can work four or five times quicker than a blunt one. Likewise, a can opener that works first time will save minutes and will keep stress levels at a minimum! A grater that you can hold comfortably, has many slicing options, and most importantly, that is sharp, will feel like a help rather than a hindrance. And we highly recommend buying yourself a good-quality food processor; whizzing up pastes and soups and chopping fruits and nuts will suddenly seem as easy as pie and you will wonder why on earth you didn't buy one before!

Easy Ingredients

There are a whole array of tasty, wonderful foods that lend themselves to fast, tasty, nutritious suppers.

Eggs, for a start, are a smart choice for a busy cook, being hugely versatile and taking a few minutes to cook. The key is to buy well—organic or farm-bought eggs really do tend to have a greater intensity of flavor and a richer color—and to blend them with exciting ingredients that will give them a whole new lease of life. Check out our Feta, Pepper, and Cherry Tomato Frittata on page 24 or the Bacon, Onion, and Egg Pan-Cooked Tart on page 90 for new ways with eggs.

Noodles are another super-easy food that are ludicrously fast to cook and can be added to soups or stir-fries after only 3 or 4 minutes cooking. Like eggs, the key is to add plenty of "easy" flavor. Coconut milk and fresh cilantro are wonderful in Thai-style soups, and garlic, chilies, ginger, Chinese 5-spice, and soy sauce are must-haves for successful stir-fries. And when time is really short, why not keep a handful of stir-in sauces in your kitchen cabinet? It may seem like cheating, but surely a freshly prepared soup or stir-fry of wholesome vegetables, noodles, and protein with a store-bought paste or sauce is better for your family than a frozen ready-meal or an expensive, calorie-laden take out?

When buying meat such as beef or lamb, be aware that the cheaper the cut of meat, often the tougher it is and therefore the longer cooking time it needs. Use frying steak or lamb chops, chicken breast or boneless thighs, and when buying pork, choose thin cuts with little or no fat. Cut all the meat you use really thinly so it cooks through quickly and easily without becoming tough in the pan.

When time allows, it is always advisable to feed your family whole grains and whole-wheat versions of their usual favorite carbs. However, do be aware that brown rice can take up to 30 minutes to cook and brown pasta always takes a little longer to cook than white pasta. We suggest buying "easy cook" versions of wholefoods wherever possible, and to speed up the process of cooking pasta and rice, use kettle-boiled water. Don't try and heat cold water on the burner—you will add a good 5 minutes to your overall cooking time!

Lastly, don't feel afraid to go to the preserved vegetables section in the supermarket and stock up on jars of chargrilled artichokes, olives, roasted tomatoes, stuffed peppers, and other interesting vegetables in flavored oils. Adding these to pasta, rice, and salads is a guaranteed easy way of adding flavor, color, and interest to your family's supper.

Easy Flavor
Many stews, roasts, and bakes infuse and develop their flavors through their long cooking times but at the end of a busy day, you don't have 2 or 3 hours to cook supper. Therefore to create the same intensity of flavors when cooking meals in a quarter of the usual cooking time, you need to ensure you use "easy flavor." By this we mean foods that give intense and almost instant taste. So stock your cabinets with garlic paste (usually found alongside tomato paste in the supermarket), ready-chopped fresh ginger and lemon grass paste; a good selection of dried herbs and spices; soy sauce; coconut milk; different types of mustards; Tabasco sauce; bouillon cubes; and preserved lemon juice. In your refrigerator, it cannot hurt to keep in some tasty, preserved meats such as chorizo and prosciutto alongside fresh onions, fresh garlic, reduced-fat feta cheese, and all your favorite colorful, crunchy vegetables.

Winter Warmers

Welcoming recipes for cold winter days.

Pea, Mint, and Bacon Soup with Sour Cream 26

Mushroom and Thyme Soup with Goat Cheese Croûtes 38

Cauliflower Cheese Soup 56

One-Pan Chicken with Honeyed Roots and Stuffing 78

Tray-Baked Sausages with Apples and Onions 86

Turkey Meatballs in Rich Tomato and Herb Sauce 114

Mixed Mushroom Stroganoff 194

Tomato, Rosemary, and Cannellini Bean Stew 200

Penne with Pan-Fried Butternut Squash and Pesto 204

Raspberry Rice Brûlée 240

Pear and Chocolate Crumble 238

Treacle Sponge Microwave Puddings 264

One of Your 5-a-Day

Tasty meals using seasonal fruit and vegetables.

Eggplant and Garlic Dip with Toasted Pita 52

Mango and Spinach Salad with Warm Peanut Chicken 72

Lamb and Tray-Roasted Vegetables with Chickpeas 112

Thai Vegetable Curry 182

Lemon Mixed Vegetable Kebabs with Nut Pilaff 192

Goat Cheese and Spinach Risotto 198

Fruity Chickpea Tagine with Cilantro Couscous 208

Vegetable, Fruit, and Nut Biryani 212

Butternut Squash, Tomato, and Red Onion Gratin 222

Warm Spiced Plums with Ice Cream 244

Rhubarb and Ginger Tartlets 258

Griddled Madeira Cake with Fruit Compote 262

Weekend Treats

Delicious recipes to indulge you and your family.

Salami and Corn Hash with Poached Eggs 36

Fried Eggy Bread Sandwich with Mozzarella 48

Corn Fritters with Chili and Tomato Salsa 50

Eggs Florentine 54

Beef Tenderloin with Mustard Crust and Oven Fries 74

Apricot-Glazed Ham Steaks with Paprika Potatoes 92

Roasted Smoked Haddock with Mash and Poached Eggs 170

Spicy Bean Burgers with Tomato Salsa 184

Coconut Dahl with Toasted Naan Fingers 224

Chocolate and Raspberry Layers 234

Make-Ahead Cheesecakes with Berry Compote 236

Chocolate Mousse with Pistachio Ice Cream 250

Healthy Midweek Meals

Great-tasting low-fat meals everyone will enjoy.

Thai Chicken Soup 46

Chargrilled Chicken with Salsa and Fruity Couscous 64

Sweet and Sour Pork with Fresh Pineapple Chunks 66

Asian-Style Beef Skewers with Satay Sauce 110

Poached Chicken with Thai Red Curry Sauce 124

Creamy Scallops with Leeks 144

Lemony Shrimp and Broccoli Stir-Fry 154

Cherry Tomato and Cod Stir-Fry with Bacon 172

Sticky Honey and Chili Salmon Skewers with Rice 174

Egg, Basil, and Cheese Salad with Cherry Tomatoes 188

Puy Lentil Stew with Garlic and Herb Bread 226

Oat-Topped Orchard Fruit Crumbles 254

Kids' Favorites

Always a winner with the little ones.

Creamy Ham and Mustard Pasta 42

Artichoke, Olive, and Taleggio Mini Pizzas 58

Sausage, Rosemary, and Mixed Bean Hotpot 70

Mushroom and Cheese Burgers with Cucumber Salsa 98

Crispy Cod Goujons with Lime and Caper Mayonnaise 136

Tuna Pasta Gratin with Butternut Squash and Peas 142

Pan-Fried Cod and Fries with Lemon Mayo and Dill 160

Cheesy Tuna and Corn Fishcakes 164

Roasted Vegetable Pasta with Garlic and Herb Sauce 186

Banoffee Layers 252

Chocolate Puddle Pudding 266

Caramel Bananas 276

Straight From The Pan

Try something new with these one-pot wonders.

Feta, Pepper, and Cherry Tomato Frittata 24

Coconut Soup with Spinach and Butternut Squash 34

Special Fried Rice 84

Bacon, Onion, and Egg Pan-Cooked Tart 90

Rustic Lamb and Potato Curry 96

Smoky Chicken and Shrimp Paella 106

Sticky Ham Steaks with Caramelized Onions 118

Salmon with Green Vegetables 132

Cajun Spiced Salmon Frittata with Peppers 166

Chunky Vegetable Red Lentil Dahl 216

Cauliflower and Potato Curry with Spinach 220

Coconut Dahl with Toasted Naan Fingers 224

Special Occasions

For when the family deserve something special.

Chicken Thighs with Lemon Sour Cream and Greens 88

Coq au Vin-Style Chicken Breasts 94

Stir-Fried Duck with Sugar Snaps and Orange Rice 102

Lamb Fillet with Mushroom and Spinach Sauce 104

Pork Scallops with Prosciutto 116

Prosciutto and Pesto-Wrapped Angler Fish 138

Creamy Haddock Gratin 150

Black Olive and Sunblush Tomato Risotto with Cod 176

Spinach, Pine Nut, and Cheese Phyllo Pie 210

White Chocolate Cream with Raspberries 242

Caramel Pear Tart Tatin 268

Quick Tiramisu with Strawberries 278

Taste of Summer

Recipes packed with the fresh flavors of summer.

Crisp-Fried Citrusy Calamari with Chili Sauce 40

Brie, Pepper, and Spinach Deep-Set Frittata 44

Chicken and Tarragon Burgers 68

Chicken and Chorizo Jambalaya with Peppers 76

Spicy Cajun Chicken Quinoa with Dried Apricots 100

Parmesan-Crusted Haddock with Tomato Avocado Salsa 130

Jamaican Spiced Salmon with Corn and Okra 156

Garlic and Tomato Seafood Spaghetti 162

Broiled Haloumi with Warm Couscous Salad 202

Apricots with Lemon Cream and Soft Amaretti 246

Pan-Fried Pineapple with Rum and Raisins 256

Scone, Strawberry, and Clotted Cream Trifles 270

QuickCook

Snacks, Appetizers, and Light Bites

Recipes listed by cooking time

30

20

10

20 Feta, Pepper, and Cherry Tomato Frittata

Serves 4

3 tablespoons olive oil
1 red bell pepper, cored, seeded, and cut into chunks
1 red onion, roughly chopped
¾ cup cherry tomatoes, halved
6 eggs
7 oz feta cheese, drained and crumbled
handful of arugula leaves
salt and pepper

- Heat 2 tablespoons of the oil in a 9 inch nonstick skillet and cook the red pepper and onion over medium heat, stirring occasionally, for 5 minutes until softened. Add the tomatoes and cook, stirring, for 2 minutes.

- Beat the eggs in a bowl and season with plenty of salt and pepper, then pour over the vegetable mixture in the pan. Sprinkle with the feta and cook over low heat for 4–5 minutes until the base of the frittata is set.

- Place the pan under a preheated medium broiler, making sure that the pan handle is turned away from the heat, and cook for 3–4 minutes until the top is golden and set. Remove from the broiler, sprinkle the arugula over the center of the frittata and season with a good grinding of pepper. Drizzle with the remaining tablespoon of oil and serve cut into wedges.

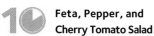

1 Feta, Pepper, and Cherry Tomato Salad

Toss together 1 red bell pepper, cored, seeded, and cut into chunks, 1 chopped red onion, ¾ cup cherry tomatoes, halved, and 7 oz crumbled feta cheese in a bowl with ½ cup pitted black olives and 2 cups arugula leaves. Whisk together the juice of 1 lemon, 4 tablespoons olive oil, and 2 tablespoons chopped parsley in a small bowl, and toss with the salad before serving.

3 Sausage, Pepper, and Cherry Tomato Frittata

Heat 1 tablespoon olive oil in a 9 inch nonstick skillet and cook 4 chorizo-style pork sausages over medium heat, turning frequently, for 8–10 minutes until browned all over and cooked through. Remove and thickly slice. Heat 2 tablespoons olive oil in the pan and cook 1 red bell pepper, cored, seeded, and cut into chunks, and 1 chopped red onion over medium heat, stirring occasionally, for 5 minutes.

Add the sliced sausages and ¾ cup cherry tomatoes, halved, and cook, stirring, for 2 minutes. Beat 6 eggs in a bowl and season with plenty of salt and pepper, then pour over the mixture in the pan. Cook over low heat for 4–5 minutes until the base is set. Place the pan under a preheated medium broiler, making sure that the pan handle is turned away from the heat, and cook for 3–4 minutes until the top is golden and set.

30 Pea, Mint, and Bacon Soup with Sour Cream

Serves 4

2 tablespoons olive oil
1 onion, roughly chopped
6 Canadian bacon slices, chopped
4 tablespoons chopped mint
1 ⅓ cups chopped, peeled
   potatoes
3 cups frozen peas
5 cups chicken stock
4 tablespoons sour cream
salt and pepper
roasted mixed seeds, to serve

- Heat the oil in a large, heavy saucepan and cook the onion and bacon over medium heat, stirring frequently, for 5 minutes until the onion is softened and the bacon browned. Add the mint and potatoes and cook, stirring, for 1 minute, then add the peas and stock. Bring to a boil, then reduce the heat, cover, and simmer for 15 minutes until the potatoes are tender.

- Transfer the soup in 2 batches to a food processor and whiz until smooth. Return to the pan, swirl in the sour cream and heat through for 1 minute.

- Season with a little salt and pepper, then ladle into warmed serving bowls and sprinkle with roasted seeds to serve.

---

10 Up-Styled Store-Bought Pea and Mint Soup Warm through 2½ cups ready-made fresh pea and mint soup in a saucepan. Meanwhile, chop 4 pancetta slices. Heat 1 tablespoon olive oil in a skillet and cook the pancetta with a handful of torn focaccia bread over high heat until crisp and golden. Serve the soup ladled into warmed bowls with the pancetta and bread sprinkled on top.

---

20 Summer Pea Soup with Feta and Pesto Toasts Heat 2 tablespoons olive oil in a large, heavy saucepan and cook 1 chopped onion and 1 chopped garlic clove over medium heat, stirring frequently, for 5 minutes. Add 3 cups frozen petit pois and 5 cups chicken stock. Bring to a boil, then simmer for 5 minutes. Transfer in 2 batches to a food processor and whiz until smooth. Return to the pan, stir in 4 tablespoons sour cream, season, and heat through for 1 minute. Meanwhile, cut 8 slices from a crusty white loaf and toast under a preheated high broiler on one side only. Top the untoasted sides with 7 oz drained, crumbled feta cheese and dot with 2 tablespoons green pesto. Toast for an additional 3 minutes or until golden. Ladle the soup into warmed bowls and serve 2 toasts with each.

30 Roasted Indian Sweet Potato Wedges with Raita

Serves 4

2 teaspoons cumin seeds
2 teaspoons coriander seeds
½ teaspoon fenugreek seeds
2 tablespoons sunflower oil
2 x 10 oz packages ready-prepared sweet potato wedges
¼ teaspoon dried red pepper flakes
salt and pepper

For the raita

¾ cup plain whole milk yogurt
4 tablespoons chopped mint
¼ cucumber, finely diced

- Place all the spices in a small, heavy skillet and cook over high heat for 1 minute, swirling the pan to toast the seeds evenly. Transfer to a mortar and grind with a pestle until finely ground. Mix the ground spices with the oil, then toss with the sweet potato wedges in a large bowl.

- Spread the wedges out in a large roasting pan, season with salt and pepper, and sprinkle with the pepper flakes. Place in a preheated oven, 400°F, for 20 minutes until beginning to brown. Meanwhile, mix together the ingredients for the raita and place in a small serving bowl.

- Remove the roasted sweet potato wedges from the oven and serve with the raita for dipping.

1 Sweet Potato Chips Heat 1¼ cups vegetable oil in a deep, heavy-based saucepan to 350–375°F, or until a cube of bread browns in 30 seconds. Meanwhile, thinly slice 2 peeled sweet potatoes with a mandolin or vegetable peeler. Deep-fry in small batches for 1–2 minutes until browned. Remove with a slotted spoon and drain on paper towels. Sprinkle with sea salt and cumin seeds. Serve with a 6¾ oz jar raita and some prepared fresh vegetables cut into chunks for dipping.

2 Roasted Indian-Style Sweet Potato and Squash Toss 2¼ cups ready-prepared diced butternut squash and sweet potato with 2 tablespoons korma curry paste and 2 tablespoons plain yogurt in a large bowl. Spread out in a large roasting pan and place in a preheated oven, 425°F, for 15 minutes. Meanwhile, make the raita as above and serve alongside the roasted vegetables.

Smoked Salmon, Cream Cheese, and Chive Omelet

Serves 4

2 tablespoons vegetable oil
6 eggs, beaten
7 oz cream cheese
1 tablespoon cold water
4 oz smoked salmon pieces
3 tablespoons snipped chives
salt and pepper
salad, to serve (optional)

- Heat the oil in a large, heavy skillet. Season the eggs with salt and pepper, then pour into the pan and cook over gentle heat for 4–5 minutes until the base is set and the top is almost set.

- Meanwhile, beat the cream cheese in a bowl with the measurement water until very soft.

- Spoon the cheese over the omelet and gently spread a little. Arrange the smoked salmon over the top, then sprinkle with the chives and cook gently for 1 minute more until the top is warm.

- Fold one side of the omelet over the other. Serve cut into 4 wedges, with a simple salad, if desired.

 Smoked Salmon and Chive Mini Soufflés Melt 1 tablespoon butter in a saucepan, add 2 tablespoons all-purpose flour, and cook over medium heat, stirring, for a few seconds. Remove from the heat and add ⅔ cup milk, a little at a time, blending well between each addition. Return to the heat, then bring to a boil, stirring constantly, cooking until thickened. Stir in 2 oz roughly chopped smoked salmon, 1 tablespoon finely chopped chives, and salt and pepper. Whisk 2 eggs in a grease-free bowl until stiff peaks form, then gently fold into the sauce. Divide between 4 individual ramekins, place on a baking sheet, and bake in a preheated oven, 400°F, for 10 minutes until golden and puffed. Serve immediately.

Baked Smoked Salmon, Pea, and Dill Tortilla Squares Beat 6 eggs in a bowl with 4 tablespoons chopped dill weed, and plenty of pepper. Stir in 4 oz snipped smoked salmon and ⅔ cup frozen peas, then pour into a lightly greased 8 inch square cake pan. Place in a preheated oven, 400°F, for 20–25 minutes until browned in places and firm to the touch. Cut into chunky squares to serve.

3○ Crispy Chili Beef with Vegetables

Serves 4

vegetable oil, for deep-frying and stir-frying
2 eggs
2 tablespoons cornstarch
10 oz frying steak, thinly sliced into strips
2 carrots, peeled and shredded
1 bunch of scallions, shredded
1 cup sugar snap peas, halved
1 red chili, sliced
2 tablespoons superfine sugar
4 tablespoons rice vinegar
4 tablespoons sweet chili sauce
1 tablespoon light soy sauce

- Fill a deep, heavy saucepan one-quarter full with vegetable oil and heat to 350–375°F, or until a cube of bread browns in 30 seconds. Meanwhile, beat together the eggs and cornstarch thoroughly in a bowl. Add the beef strips and toss to coat.

- Deep-fry the beef strips in 2 batches, lowering them into the oil with a slotted spoon and cooking for 10 seconds before stirring to prevent the strips from sticking together. Continue to cook for 5 minutes until golden and crisp. Remove with the slotted spoon and drain on paper towels.

- Heat 1 tablespoon oil in a large wok or heavy skillet over high heat and stir-fry the carrots, scallions, sugar snap peas, and chili for 2–3 minutes until softened. Add the sugar, rice vinegar, and sweet chili and soy sauces, mix well, and cook for 1 minute. Add the beef to the pan and toss well, then serve immediately.

 1 Chili Beef and Red Pepper Stir-Fry

Slice 10 oz frying steak. Heat 1 tablespoon sesame oil in a large wok or heavy skillet and stir-fry the steak with 1 seeded and finely chopped red chili and 1 red bell pepper, cored, seeded, and cut into matchsticks, for 3 minutes. Add 2 tablespoons oyster sauce and cook for 1 minute more. Serve on a bed of cooked plain rice and sprinkle with 1 tablespoon chopped chives.

 2 Quick Crispy Chili Beef with Broccoli

Thinly slice 10 oz thin-cut sirloin steaks and toss with 3 tablespoons seasoned cornstarch. Heat 4 tablespoons sesame oil and 2 tablespoons vegetable oil in a large wok or heavy skillet and stir-fry the beef over high heat for 3–4 minutes until crisp. Remove from the pan with a slotted spoon. Add 1 large head sliced broccoli florets, 1 large carrot, cut into thick batons, 2 sliced garlic cloves, 2 teaspoons peeled and chopped fresh ginger root, and ½ teaspoon dried red pepper flakes and stir-fry for 3–4 minutes until softened. Add 4 tablespoons light soy sauce mixed with 2 tablespoons sugar and 2 tablespoons sweet chili sauce, toss well, and cook for 1 minute. Return the beef to the pan with 1 bunch of roughly chopped scallions and heat through. Serve with ready-cooked long-grain rice, heated through according to the package instructions.

 Coconut Soup with Spinach and Butternut Squash

Serves 4

1 tablespoon vegetable oil

1 onion, finely chopped

1 lb butternut squash, peeled, seeded, and cut into cubes

1 small red chili, finely chopped

1 teaspoon ground coriander

1½ cups canned coconut milk

2½ cups rich chicken or vegetable stock

6 cups spinach leaves

warm naan breads, to serve

- Heat the oil in a large, heavy saucepan and cook the onion, butternut squash, and chili over medium-high heat, stirring frequently, for 8 minutes until softened. Add the coriander and cook, stirring, for a few seconds, then stir in the coconut milk and stock and bring to a boil. Reduce the heat and simmer for 10 minutes.

- Stir in the spinach leaves and cook for 1 minute until just wilted. Ladle the soup into warmed serving bowls and serve with warm naan breads.

 Quick Caribbean-Style Coconut Soup

Heat 1 tablespoon vegetable oil in a large, heavy saucepan and cook 1 finely chopped red onion over medium-high heat, stirring frequently, for 3 minutes. Add 1 teaspoon ground coriander and ½ teaspoon smoked paprika and cook, stirring, for a few seconds. Stir in a 1½ cups canned coconut milk and 2½ cups chicken or vegetable stock and bring to a boil. Add a 13 oz can drained kidney beans with 6 cups spinach leaves and simmer for 5 minutes. Serve with corn bread, if desired.

 Chicken, Butternut, and Coconut Noodle Soup

Heat 1 tablespoon vegetable oil in a large, heavy saucepan and cook 8 oz minced chicken over medium-high heat, stirring to break up the meat, for 5 minutes until browned. Add 1 chopped onion, 1 lb butternut squash, peeled, seeded, and cut into cubes, 1 finely chopped small red chili and a 1 inch piece peeled and grated fresh ginger root. Cook, stirring frequently, for 8 minutes. Add 1 teaspoon ground coriander and cook, stirring, for a few seconds, then stir in 1½ cups canned coconut milk and 2½ cups chicken stock. Bring to a boil, then simmer for 10 minutes, adding 10 oz ready-cooked Thai rice noodles for the last 3 minutes of cooking time. Serve immediately.

30 Salami and Corn Hash with Poached Eggs

Serves 4

1 lb ready-prepared potato
  wedges
2 tablespoons olive oil
1 red onion, roughly chopped
1 teaspoon smoked paprika
6 oz chunk salami (from the deli
  counter), cut into chunks
1½ cups frozen corn kernels
6 tablespoons chopped parsley
4 eggs
salt

- Bring a saucepan of lightly salted water to a boil and cook the potato wedges for 5 minutes, then drain. Meanwhile, heat the oil in a large, heavy skillet and cook the onion over medium heat, stirring frequently, for 5 minutes until softened.

- Add the smoked paprika and drained potato wedges to the onion and toss well, then cook for an additional 5 minutes, stirring and breaking up to crisp and brown a little. Add the salami and corn and cook, stirring, for 3–4 minutes before adding the parsley. Toss well and then press the mixture down a little. Reduce the heat, cover, and cook for 2–3 minutes.

- While the hash is cooking, half-fill a skillet with boiling water and return to a boil. Break the eggs into the water, 2 at a time, and cook for 2 minutes until just cooked. Remove from the pan with a slotted spoon or fish spatula.

- Spoon the hash onto warmed serving plates and top each serving with a poached egg.

---

10 **Salami and Thyme Rosti with Poached Eggs** Gently break up 13 oz ready-prepared potato rosti in a bowl. Add 3 oz sliced salami, 1 grated onion, 2 tablespoons melted butter, and a few thyme leaves. Season with salt and pepper and mix well. Heat a nonstick skillet, tip in the mixture, and press down with a spatula. Cook over high heat for 4 minutes on each side until browned. Meanwhile, poach 4 eggs as above and serve on top of the rosti.

 20 **Salami and Red Pepper Hash with Baked Eggs** Parboil 10 oz thinly sliced new potatoes in a saucepan for 5 minutes, then drain. Meanwhile, heat 2 tablespoons olive oil in a large skillet and cook 1 chopped onion over medium heat, stirring frequently, for 3 minutes. Add the potato slices and ½ teaspoon dried red pepper flakes and cook, stirring and breaking up the potatoes, for 4 minutes until browned. Add 6 oz salami, cut into chunks, and ½ cup chopped flame-roasted red peppers from a jar. Mix well, then press the mixture down and cook for an additional 3 minutes before sprinkling over a handful of snipped chives. Make 4 hollows in the vegetable mixture and crack an egg into each. Cook gently for 4 minutes. Take the pan to the table and serve.

Mushroom and Thyme Soup with Goat Cheese Croûtes

Serves 4

3 tablespoons olive oil

1 onion, chopped

1 lb brown mushrooms, trimmed and roughly chopped

2 tablespoons thyme leaves, plus extra to garnish

2½ cups chicken or vegetable stock

2 tablespoons Dijon mustard plus 1 teaspoon

¾ cup sour cream

8 thin slices of small French baguette, toasted

8 thin slices of rinded goat cheese

salt and pepper

- Heat the oil in a large, heavy saucepan and cook the onion over medium heat, stirring occasionally, for 3 minutes. Add the mushrooms and thyme leaves and cook, stirring occasionally, for 5 minutes until the mushrooms are tender and browned. Pour in the stock, add the 2 tablespoons mustard, and bring to a boil. Reduce the heat and simmer for 5 minutes.

- Transfer the soup to a food processor and whiz until almost smooth, then return to the pan, add the sour cream, and season generously with a little salt and some pepper. Heat through for 1 minute.

- Thinly spread the baguette slices with the remaining teaspoon of mustard and place a goat cheese slice on top of each. Cook under a preheated high broiler for 1–2 minutes until the cheese is just beginning to brown in places.

- Serve the soup ladled into warmed serving bowls with the croûtes on top, garnished with extra thyme leaves.

 Mushroom and Thyme Ciabatta Toasts Heat 3 tablespoons olive oil in a large, heavy saucepan and cook 1 chopped onion over medium heat, stirring occasionally, for 3 minutes. Add 1 lb trimmed and roughly chopped button mushrooms and 2 tablespoons thyme leaves and cook, stirring occasionally, for 5 minutes until the mushrooms are tender and browned.

Stir in 2 tablespoons whole grain mustard and ¾ cup sour cream. Toast 4 large slices of ciabatta bread under a preheated broiler until golden, spoon one-quarter of the mushroom mixture over each toast, and garnish with thyme leaves.

 Rich Mushroom and Thyme Soup Soak ⅔ cup mixed dried mushrooms in 2½ cups hot water for 10 minutes, then drain the mushrooms and use the mushroom soaking liquid in place of the chicken stock in the recipe above. Chop the reconstituted mixed mushrooms and add to the onion with the fresh mushrooms and thyme leaves as above.

3 ⦿ Crisp-Fried Citrusy Calamari with Chili Sauce

Serves 4

vegetable oil, for deep-frying

1 lb squid rings, defrosted if frozen

⅔ cup cornstarch

2 eggs

finely grated zest and juice of 1 lime

2 tablespoons finely chopped fresh cilantro, plus extra to garnish

lime wedges, to serve

8 tablespoons sweet chili sauce

salt and pepper

- Fill a large, deep heavy saucepan one-third full with vegetable oil and heat to 350–375°F, or until a cube of bread browns in 30 seconds.

- Drain the squid rings very well. Place the cornstarch on a plate and season well with salt and pepper. Toss the calamari in the seasoned cornstarch and place on a separate plate.

- Beat the eggs thoroughly in a bowl, then add the lime zest and coriander and beat again. Beat in 2 tablespoons of the seasoned cornstarch. Dip the squid rings in the batter to coat, quickly add to the hot oil, and deep-fry in 2–3 batches, depending on the size of the pan, for 3–4 minutes until golden and crisp. Remove with a slotted spoon and drain on paper towels. Meanwhile, mix the lime juice with the chili sauce and place in a small serving bowl.

- Serve the calamari hot, sprinkled with cilantro to garnish, with lime wedges and the chili sauce for dipping.

---

1 ⦿ Pan-Fried Garlicky and Citrusy Calamari

Melt 1 tablespoon butter with 2 tablespoons olive oil in a large, heavy skillet and cook 1 sliced garlic clove with 1 lb squid rings, defrosted if frozen, over very high heat, stirring frequently, for 5 minutes until piping hot and browned in places. Finely grate the rind of 1 lemon, add to the pan along with its juice, and toss into the squid. Season generously with pepper and then sprinle with 4 tablespoons chopped parsley to serve.

2 ⦿ Spicy and Citrusy Crisp-Fried Shrimp

Mix together 2 cups fresh white bread crumbs, ½ teaspoon dried red pepper flakes, 3 teaspoons ground cumin, the finely grated zest of 1 lime, and ½ teaspoon each salt and pepper. Spread over a plate. Toss 20 large, raw, shelled but tail-on shrimp in 2 tablespoons seasoned flour on a plate, then dip into 1 beaten egg and finally into the bread crumb mixture. Heat 1½ inches vegetable oil in a large, deep heavy skillet to 350–375°F, or until a cube of bread browns in 30 seconds. Fry the shrimp in batches for 2 minutes until crisp and golden. Remove with a slotted spoon and drain on paper towels. Serve with a bowl of mayonnaise mixed with the juice from the lime and a handful of chopped fresh cilantro.

 # Creamy Ham and Mustard Pasta

Serves 4

12 oz dried fusilli
1 tablespoon olive oil
2 tablespoons butter
1 onion, thinly sliced
3½ tablespoons all-purpose flour
1¼ cups milk
1 tablespoon whole grain mustard
1 teaspoon Dijon mustard
¾ cup sour cream
8 oz smoked ham, cut into thin
  strips
4 tablespoons chopped parsley
pepper
arugula salad, to serve (optional)

- Bring a large saucepan of lightly salted water to a boil and cook the pasta for 10–12 minutes until just tender. Drain, return to the pan, and toss with the oil.

- Meanwhile, melt the butter in a large, heavy saucepan and cook the onion over medium heat, stirring occasionally, for 5 minutes until softened. Add the flour and cook, stirring, for a few seconds. Remove from the heat and add the milk, a little at a time, blending well between each addition. Return to the heat, then bring to a boil, stirring constantly, cooking until thickened.

- Stir in the mustards, sour cream, ham, and parsley and heat for 1 minute more until the sauce is piping hot but not boiling. Stir in the pasta and season with pepper.

- Serve in warmed serving bowls with a simple arugula salad, if desired.

 ### Instant Ham and Mustard Pasta

Bring a large saucepan of lightly salted water to a boil, add 1 lb fresh linguine, and cook for 3 minutes or until just tender. Drain the pasta and return to the hot pan. Stir in 8 oz smoked ham, cut into thin strips, 1 tablespoon whole grain mustard, 1 teaspoon Dijon mustard, 4 tablespoons chopped parsley, and ⅔ cup heavy cream, toss well, and serve immediately.

Ham, Mustard, and Tomato Bake

Make the recipe above, but instead of serving in warmed bowls, pour the pasta mix into a baking dish, top with 3 large, sliced beef tomatoes, and sprinkle with ½ cup grated cheddar cheese. Cook under a preheated medium broiler for 7 minutes until the tomatoes are softened and the cheese is bubbling and browned.

Brie, Spicy Pepper, and Spinach Deep-Set Frittata

Serves 4–6

3 tablespoons olive oil

1 red onion, sliced

4¼ cups baby spinach leaves

8 eggs

½ cup drained Peppadew peppers, roughly chopped

6 oz Brie, cut into chunks

salt and pepper

leafy salad, to serve (optional)

- Heat the oil in a 10 inch, heavy skillet and cook the onion over medium heat, stirring occasionally, for 5 minutes until softened. Add the spinach and cook, stirring, for 1 minute until wilted. Remove the pan from the heat.

- Beat the eggs in a bowl and season with a little salt and plenty of pepper, then pour over the spinach and onion in the pan.

- Sprinkle over the Peppadew peppers and Brie evenly and allow them to settle in the frittata mixture. Return the frittata to low heat and cook for 3–5 minutes until the base is set.

- Place the pan under a preheated medium broiler, making sure that the pan handle is turned away from the heat, and cook for 3–4 minutes until the top is golden and set. Serve cut into wedges, accompanied by a simple leafy salad, if desired.

Brie, Spicy Pepper, and Bacon Omelet

Heat ½ tablespoon olive oil in a large skillet. Snip 6 good-quality Canadian back bacon slices into small pieces and cook over medium-high heat, stirring frequently, for 3 minutes until crispy. Beat together 4 eggs, season, and pour into the pan. Cook for 1 minute, then add ½ cup drained Peppadew peppers, cut into chunks. Sprinkle with 1 tablespoon chopped chives, then sprinkle with 4 oz Brie, cut into small pieces. Cook for an additional 4–5 minutes until just set. Serve with a crusty baguette and cold French butter.

Spicy Pepper and Pea Tortilla

Heat 1 tablespoon olive oil in a large skillet and cook 1 chopped onion and ½ cup drained Peppadew peppers, roughly chopped, over medium heat, stirring occasionally, for 5 minutes. Add 1 crushed garlic clove, a drained 13 oz can lima beans, and 2 tablespoons frozen peas and cook, stirring, for 3 minutes. Beat 6 eggs in a bowl, season, and pour over the vegetable mixture in the pan. Sprinkle with 1 tablespoon chopped parsley and cook over low heat for 5 minutes. Place the pan under a preheated medium broiler, making sure that the pan handle is turned away from the heat, and cook for 3–4 minutes until lightly browned. Allow to cool for 2 minutes before cutting into thick wedges to serve.

 # Thai Chicken Soup

Serves 4

3¼ cups canned reduced-fat coconut milk

½ cup hot chicken stock

1 tablespoon Thai red curry paste

2 boneless, chicken breasts, about 6 oz each, very thinly sliced

2 cups snow peas

2 cups bean sprouts

- Place the coconut milk, stock, and curry paste in a large saucepan and bring to a boil.

- Add the chicken and cook for 2 minutes, then add the snow peas and bean sprouts and cook for an additional 5 minutes until the chicken is cooked through.

- Serve ladled into warmed serving bowls.

 Thai Green Curry Stir-Fry Heat 2 tablespoons vegetable oil in a large wok or heavy skillet and cook 1 roughly chopped lemon grass stalk, ½ inch piece of fresh ginger root, peeled and roughly chopped, and 4 thinly sliced boneless, skinless chicken breasts, about 5 oz each, over medium-high heat, stirring frequently, for 5 minutes until browned and cooked through. Add 2 cups snow peas, 1 cored, seeded, and roughly chopped red bell pepper, and 2 cups bean sprouts and stir-fry over high heat for 2–3 minutes. Blend 1 tablespoon Thai green curry paste with 6 tablespoons coconut milk, then pour over the stir-fry and cook, tossing, for another 2 minutes.

Chicken and Snow Pea Thai Green Curry Place 3¼ cups canned coconut milk in a saucepan with 1 roughly chopped lemon grass stalk and a 1 inch piece of fresh ginger root, peeled and chopped, 2 roughly chopped fresh kaffir lime leaves, 1 tablespoon Thai green curry paste, 4 boneless, skinless chicken breasts, about 5 oz each, cut into chunks, 1 cup snow peas, and 2 cored roughly chopped red bell peppers. Bring to a boil and then simmer for 15–20 minutes. Blend 2 tablespoons cornflour with 2 tablespoons cold water. Remove the pan from the heat and stir in the cornstarch mixture. Return to the heat and bring to a boil, stirring, until thickened. Add 8 tablespoons chopped cilantro and serve.

30 Fried Eggy Bread Sandwich with Mozzarella

Serves 4

4 eggs
8 slices of good-quality seeded bread
2 tablespoons vegetable oil
4 tablespoons olive oil
1 eggplant, trimmed and thinly sliced
5 oz mozzarella cheese, drained and thinly sliced into 12 slices
handful of spinach leaves
4 tablespoons red pesto
salt and pepper

- Beat the eggs in a large shallow bowl and season with a little salt and pepper. Dip the bread slices into the beaten egg until coated on both sides. Heat the vegetable oil in a large, heavy skillet and cook the bread in batches over medium-high heat for 30 seconds–1 minute on each side until golden and set. Remove and stack to keep warm.

- Heat the olive oil in the pan and cook the eggplant slices over medium-high heat for 5–6 minutes, turning once, until browned and tender. Remove and keep warm.

- To assemble, divide the eggplant slices between 4 of the eggy bread slices, cover each with 3 mozzarella slices then top with a few spinach leaves. Spread the remaining eggy bread slices with the pesto and place, pesto-side down, on each stack. Press down well. Return to the warm pan and cook over low heat for 2 minutes, turning once, until the spinach has wilted and the mozzarella begins to melt. Cut each sandwich in half diagonally and serve warm.

 Brie and Pine Nut Eggy Bread with Salsa Butter 8 slices of good-quality bread, top the buttered side of 4 bread slices with a thick slice of Brie and sprinkle with 2 tablespoons toasted pine nuts. Cover with the remaining bread slices, butter-side down, and cut in half diagonally. Beat 2 eggs with 2 tablespoons milk in a shallow bowl and season. Melt a knob of butter with 1 teaspoon olive oil in a large skillet. Dip the sandwiches in the egg mixture and cook for 2 minutes on each side. Serve with fresh salsa.

 Roasted Tomato and Pesto Eggy Bread Cut 4 tomatoes in half and place, cut-side up, in a baking dish. Top each with a basil leaf, drizzle with olive oil, and season with salt and pepper. Place in a preheated oven, 400°F, for 15 minutes. Meanwhile, mix 3 beaten eggs with 1 tablespoon milk, season, and pour into a wide dish. Spread 8 slices of good-quality bread on both sides with ready-made green pesto. Dip the bread slices into the egg mixture until coated on both sides. Heat 1 tablespoon olive oil in a large, heavy skillet and cook the bread in 2 batches over medium-high heat for 1 minute on each side. Serve the eggy bread topped with the roasted tomatoes.

Corn Fritters with Chili and Tomato Salsa

Serves 4

9 oz can corn kernels
½ cup all-purpose flour
1 teaspoon baking powder
1 egg, beaten
½ red bell pepper, finely chopped
1 small red chili, seeded, and finely
chopped
6 tablespoons chopped cilantro
2 tablespoons vegetable oil
pepper

For the salsa

1 tablespoon olive oil
2 tomatoes, finely chopped
½ small red chili, finely chopped
1 tablespoon light brown sugar
2 tablespoons chopped cilantro

- Drain the corn and place half the kernels in a food processor and whiz until almost smooth. Transfer to a bowl and stir in the remaining, whole corn. Sift in the flour and baking powder and mix together. Mix in the egg, red pepper, chili, and cilantro and season with plenty of pepper.

- Heat the vegetable oil in a large, heavy nonstick skillet over medium-high heat and drop in 4 spoonfuls of the mixture. Cook for about 1 minute on each side until browned. Remove with a spatula, drain on paper towels, and keep warm. Cook the remaining mixture in the same way (to make 8 fritters in total).

- Meanwhile, mix together all the ingredients for the salsa, season with pepper, and place in a serving bowl.

- Serve the fritters warm with the salsa on the side.

 Corn Pancakes
Make up a 5 oz package pancake batter mix according to the package instructions and mix in 8 tablespoons drained canned corn and 3 tablespoons chopped cilantro. Season well. Heat a little vegetable oil in a skillet over medium-high heat, pour in one-quarter of the mixture, and cook for 1 minute, then turn and cook for a few seconds on the other side. Cook the remaining mixture in the same way. Fill the pancakes with store-bought tomato salsa and a few arugula leaves, if desired.

 Crab and Corn Fritters Whiz half a drained 9 oz can corn kernels in a food processor until almost smooth. Spoon out the light and dark meat from a fresh dressed crab and stir into the pureed corn with the remaining, whole corn and 2 finely chopped scallions. Sift in ½ cup all-purpose flour and 1 teaspoon baking powder and mix together. Mix in 1 beaten egg, ½ finely chopped red bell pepper, 1 small seeded, and finely chopped red chili, 6 tablespoons chopped fresh cilantro, and plenty of pepper. Heat 2 tablespoons vegetable oil in a large, heavy nonstick skillet over medium-high heat and drop in 4 spoonfuls of the mixture. Cook for about 1 minute on each side until browned. Remove with a fish spatula, drain on paper towels, and keep warm. Cook the remaining mixture in the same way. Serve on salad leaves with a small bowl of salsa as above.

30 Eggplant and Garlic Dip with Toasted Pita

Serves 4

2 large eggplants
2 teaspoons ground cumin
1 teaspoon ground coriander
1 garlic clove, roughly chopped
⅔ cup olive oil
finely grated zest and juice of
  1 lemon
4 tablespoons chopped fresh
  cilantro
salt and pepper
pita breads, to serve

- Trim the eggplants, then slice lengthwise into thick slices. Mix the cumin, ground coriander, and garlic into the oil, then lightly brush both sides of each eggplant slice with the flavored oil, reserving the remaining oil.

- Heat a large, heavy skillet over medium-high heat and cook one-third of the eggplant slices for 3–4 minutes, turning once, until softened and lightly browned. Remove from the pan and cook the remaining batches of slices in the same way.

- Place the warm eggplant slices in a food processor with the lemon zest and juice and the reserved flavored oil. Whiz until almost smooth but with a little texture. Transfer to a bowl, then mix in the fresh cilantro and season with a little salt and pepper.

- Griddle or toast the pita breads until golden and warm, cut into strips, and serve with the dip.

10 Quick Baba Ganoush Dip

In a food processor, whiz together a 6 oz jar chargrilled eggplants, 2 tablespoons lemon juice, 2 tablespoons tahini, 1 chopped garlic clove, ½ teaspoon salt, and a large pinch of ground cumin to a thick puree. Taste and adjust the seasoning. Add 1 tablespoon plain yogurt and whiz again briefly for a less smoky flavor. Transfer to a serving bowl, drizzle with olive oil, and sprinkle with chopped parsley. Serve with a crisp salad.

20 Easy Caponata Dip

Heat 2 tablespoons olive oil in a large, heavy skillet and cook 1 chopped onion, 1 chopped celery stick, 1 red and 1 yellow bell pepper, cored, seeded, and chopped, and 2 sliced garlic cloves over medium heat, stirring occasionally, for 15 minutes. Add a 4 oz tub chargrilled eggplants from the deli counter, sliced into chunky pieces, a 13 oz can chopped tomatoes, 1 tablespoon small capers, a handful of chopped pitted green olives, 1 tablespoon red wine vinegar, and 1 teaspoon superfine sugar. Warm through and serve with ciabatta bread.

⏱ 10 Eggs Florentine

Serves 4

1 tablespoon butter, plus extra for buttering the muffins
4¼ cups spinach leaves
4 English muffins, split in half
4 eggs
3 tablespoons chopped parsley
¾ cup ready-made hollandaise sauce
salt and pepper

- Half-fill a small saucepan with water and bring to a boil. Meanwhile, melt the butter in a large saucepan, add the spinach, and cook over medium heat, stirring, for 1–2 minutes until wilted. Season with salt and pepper.

- Toast the muffins, cut-side up, under a preheated medium broiler until lightly browned. Meanwhile, poach the eggs, 2 at a time, in the boiling water and cook for 1–2 minutes until the whites are firm and the yolks soft.

- Butter the warm muffins, then divide the spinach between them and top with an egg. Mix the parsley into the hollandaise and spoon over the eggs. Serve with ground black pepper.

 Eggs Florentine with Leek and Cheese Sauce Melt 2 tablespoons butter in a saucepan and cook 2 finely sliced leeks over medium heat, stirring, for 3–4 minutes until soft and beginning to brown. Stir in 3½ tablespoons all-purpose flour, then remove from the heat and add 1¾ cups milk, a little at a time, blending well between each addition. Add 1 teaspoon prepared English mustard and stir well, return to the heat and bring to a boil, stirring constantly, until thickened. Stir in 2 tablespoons freshly grated Parmesan cheese. Cook and prepare the spinach, eggs, and muffins as above, then assemble with the leek and cheese sauce instead of the parsley hollandaise, serving with extra grated Parmesan, if liked.

 Baked Eggs with Spinach and Parmesan Butter Mix 7 tablespoons softened butter with 2 tablespoons drained and chopped sundried tomatoes in oil, 2 tablespoons freshly grated Parmesan cheese, and 2 tablespoons chopped basil. Melt 1 tablespoon of the flavored butter in a large saucepan and cook 8 cups spinach leaves over medium heat for 2–3 minutes until wilted. Spoon into the base of 4 large ramekin dishes, then crack an egg over the top of each. Add a small knob of the flavored butter to the top of each and place in the preheated oven, 400°F, for 12–15 minutes until set. Spread the remaining flavored butter over 8 thick slices of French baguette, place on a baking sheet, and place in the oven for the final 5–6 minutes of the cooking time until golden. Serve the baked eggs with the toasts.

Cauliflower Cheese Soup

Serves 4

1 cauliflower, trimmed and cut
into florets
2½ cups chicken stock
1¼ cups milk
2 tablespoons butter
2 leeks, trimmed, cleaned, and
finely sliced
2 teaspoons prepared English
mustard
1 teaspoon ground nutmeg
1 cup grated cheddar cheese
3 tablespoons vegetable oil
2 thick slices of white or brown
bread, roughly cut into small
cubes
½ teaspoon ground paprika
pepper

- Place the cauliflower florets in a saucepan with the stock
and milk and bring to a boil. Reduce the heat and simmer
for 10 minutes until the cauliflower is tender.

- Meanwhile, melt the butter in a heavy skillet and cook the
leeks over medium heat, stirring occasionally, for 5 minutes.

- Add the mustard and nutmeg to the cauliflower, then stir
in the cheese. Transfer to a food processor and whiz until
smooth. Return to the pan, stir in the leeks, and season
with a little pepper. Heat through gently while cooking
the croutons.

- Heat the oil in a large, heavy skillet over high heat. Toss the
bread cubes with the paprika and cook the croutons, stirring
frequently, for 2–3 minutes until golden and crisp. Remove
with a slotted spoon and drain on paper towels.

- Ladle the soup into warmed serving bowls and sprinkle the
croutons over the top.

**Speedy Spinach
and Cheese Soup**

Place 2½ cups chicken stock and
1¼ cups milk in a saucepan, add
1¼ cups frozen chopped spinach,
2 teaspoons prepared English
mustard, and 1 teaspoon ground
nutmeg and bring to a boil.
Reduce the heat and simmer for
5 minutes, then stir in a 1¼ cups
ready-made cheese sauce and
heat for 2 minutes. Serve in
warmed serving bowls with
store-bought croutons.

**Classic Cauliflower
Cheese** Place 1
cauliflower, trimmed and cut into
florets, in a saucepan of water
and bring to a boil. Reduce the
heat and simmer for 10 minutes.
Meanwhile, melt 3½ tablespoons
butter in a saucepan, add 6
tablespoons all-purpose flour,
and cook over medium heat,
stirring, for a few seconds.
Remove from the heat and add
2½ cups milk, a little at a time,
blending well between each
addition. Return to the heat,

then bring to a boil, stirring
constantly, cooking until
thickened. Beat in 1 cup grated
cheddar cheese, 2 teaspoons
prepared English mustard, and 1
teaspoon ground nutmeg. Drain
the cauliflower and place in a
baking dish, pour over the cheese
sauce, and sprinkle the top with
½ cup grated cheddar. Cook
under a preheated high broiler
for 5 minutes until browned.

Artichoke, Olive, and Taleggio Mini Pizzas

Serves 4

5 oz package pizza base mix
all-purpose flour, for dusting
4 tablespoons sundried tomato paste
9 oz jar artichoke antipasti, well drained
4 tablespoons pitted kalamata olives
4 oz taleggio cheese, sliced
arugula leaves dressed with olive oil and lemon juice, to serve (optional)

- Make up the pizza base mix according to the package instructions and divide into 4 pieces. Knead each piece briefly on a lightly floured work surface, then roll each into a 5 inch round and place on a baking sheet.

- Spread each round with 1 tablespoon of the tomato paste, then randomly sprinkle the drained artichokes and black olives over the top.

- Top with the slices of taleggio, tucked between the vegetables and placed over them. Place in a preheated oven, 425°F, for 12 minutes until the bases are cooked and the tops lightly browned.

- Serve the pizzas hot, with arugula leaves dressed with olive oil and lemon juice, if desired.

 Sundried Tomato and Artichoke Ciabatta Pizzas Slice 2 olive ciabatta loaves in half horizontally. Spread with 4 tablespoons sundried tomato paste, then randomly sprinkle a drained 8 oz jar artichoke antipasti and a handful of drained sundried tomatoes in oil over the top. Sprinkle with 5½ oz mini mozzarella balls and top with a fresh grating of Parmesan cheese. Cook under a preheated high broiler for 4–5 minutes until the cheese is lightly browned and bubbling.

Pancetta, Goat Cheese, and Artichoke Pizzas Place 2 store-bought ready-made pizza bases on a baking sheet. Spread with 2 tablespoons green pesto, then arrange a drained 8 oz jar artichoke antipasti over the top, sprinkle with 3 oz cubed pancetta, and top with 4 oz sliced goat cheese. Place in a preheated oven, 425°F, for 12 minutes. Cut each pizza in half and serve with a crunchy herb salad.

QuickCook
Meaty Suppers

Recipes listed by cooking time

10

30 Chargrilled Chicken with Salsa and Fruity Couscous

Serves 4

4 boneless, skinless chicken breasts, about 5 oz each
6 tablespoons balsamic vinegar
1 cup couscous
1½ cups boiled water, slightly cooled
3 tablespoons olive oil
1 avocado, pitted, peeled, and roughly chopped
1 large tomato, roughly chopped
5 tablespoons chopped fresh cilantro
⅓ cup raisins
4 tablespoons pumpkin seeds
salt

- Place the chicken in a nonmetallic container, pour over the vinegar, and coat. Cover and allow to marinate for 5 minutes.

- Place the couscous in a bowl, pour over the measurement water, and season with a little salt. Cover and allow to absorb the water for 10 minutes.

- Meanwhile, heat 1 tablespoon of the oil in a large skillet or griddle pan and cook the chicken over medium heat, turning once, for 10–12 minutes until browned and cooked through.

- While the chicken is cooking, make the salsa by mixing together the avocado, tomato, 1 tablespoon of the remaining olive oil, and 1 tablespoon of the cilantro in a bowl.

- Stir the remaining tablespoon of olive oil into the couscous, then add the raisins, pumpkin seeds, and remaining cilantro and toss again. Serve on warmed serving plates topped with the chicken, with the salsa spooned over.

---

 1 Sundried Tomato and Chicken Couscous Cook a 3¾ oz package tomato and onion couscous according to package instructions. Heat 3 tablespoons oil from a container sundried tomatoes in oil in a large saucepan and heat through 13 oz ready-cooked chicken breast chunks for 3 minutes. Add 5 chopped sundried tomatoes and 1 diced red bell pepper and cook over medium heat, stirring, for 5 minutes. Stir in 2 chopped scallions, 1 tablespoon each honey and balsamic vinegar, 1 teaspoon whole grain mustard, and the couscous.

 2 Chargrilled Chicken with Salsa and Lemon Couscous Cook 4 boneless, skinless chicken breasts, about 5 oz each, as above. Meanwhile, place 1 cup couscous in a bowl, then pour over 1¼ cups hot chicken stock, cover, and allow to absorb for 10 minutes. While the couscous is standing, for the salsa, mix together 1 pitted, peeled, and diced mango, 1 small finely chopped red onion, 1 chopped tomato, and 1 tablespoon chopped fresh cilantro in a serving bowl. In a separate bowl, mix together the finely grated zest and juice of 1 lemon, 1 tablespoon each olive oil, balsamic vinegar, and chopped mint, and a pinch of sugar. Pour over the couscous and mix well. Serve the couscous and salsa with the chicken as above.

Sweet and Sour Pork with Fresh Pineapple Chunks

Serves 4

1 tablespoon vegetable oil

½ pineapple, skinned, cored, and cut into bite-size chunks

1 onion, cut into chunks

1 orange bell pepper, cored, seeded, and cut into chunks

12 oz pork tenderloin, cut into strips

1 cup snow peas, halved lengthwise

6 tablespoons tomato ketchup

2 tablespoons light brown sugar

2 tablespoons white wine or malt vinegar

cooked egg noodles, to serve (optional)

- Heat the oil in a large, heavy skillet or wok and stir-fry the pineapple chunks over very high heat for 3–4 minutes until browned in places. Remove with a slotted spoon. Add the onion and orange pepper and cook over high heat, stirring frequently, for 5 minutes until softened. Add the pork strips and stir-fry for 5 minutes until browned and cooked through.

- Return the pineapple to the pan with the snow peas and cook, stirring occasionally, for 2 minutes. Mix the tomato ketchup, sugar, and vinegar together in a bowl and pour over the pork mixture. Toss and cook for 1 minute more to heat the sauce through.

- Serve immediately, with egg noodles, if desired.

Speedy Sweet and Sour Pork Stir-Fry

Drain the juice from a 14 oz can crushed pineapple and blend 5 tablespoons of juice with 2 tablespoons cornstarch, add 4 tablespoons rice vinegar and 2 tablespoons each tomato ketchup, dark soy sauce, soft light brown sugar. Heat 1 tablespoon vegetable oil in a large skillet over high heat and stir-fry 7 oz pork strips for 2 minutes. Add 1 chopped red bell pepper, stir-fry for 2 minutes, then add 5 shredded scallions, the pineapple, and the pineapple juice mixture, warm through, and serve with noodles.

Roast Sweet and Sour Pork

Mix together 5 tablespoons hoisin sauce, 2 tablespoons Chinese red cooking wine, 2 tablespoons sunflower oil, 1 tablespoon dark soy sauce, 1 ⅓ cup chopped scallions, and 3 chopped garlic cloves. Pour over 4 pork steaks, each 6 oz in weight, in an ovenproof dish, then drizzle with 1 tablespoon honey. Place in a preheated oven, 350°F, for 20 minutes. Drizzle over another tablespoon of honey and return to the oven for 5 minutes. Meanwhile, heat 1 tablespoon sesame oil in a large skillet or wok and stir-fry ½ pineapple skinned, cored, and cut into chunks, over high heat for 3 minutes. Add a handful of bok choy and stir-fry until wilted. Serve the pork over egg noodles with the pineapple and bok choy on top.

Chicken and Tarragon Burgers

Serves 4

1 lb boneless, skinless chicken
 breasts, roughly chopped
1 tablespoon whole grain mustard
3 tablespoons chopped tarragon
½ small red chili, finely chopped
 (optional)
4 whole-wheat buns
pepper

To serve

béarnaise sauce from a jar
arugula leaves tossed in lemon
 juice

- Place the chicken in a food processor and whiz until smooth. Transfer to a bowl, add the mustard, tarragon, and chili and season well with pepper. Mix together until well blended, then shape into 4 patties.

- Lay the chicken burgers on a broiler rack lined with foil and cook under a preheated high broiler for 4–5 minutes on each side until browned and cooked through. Split the buns and place, cut-side up, under the broiler for the final 1 minute of cooking time.

- Place a hot burger on the top of each warm bun base and top with a spoonful of béarnaise sauce and a handful of lemon juice-dressed arugula. Cover with the warm bun tops and serve immediately.

Crunchy Chicken Burgers with Tarragon Mayonnaise

Place 4 boneless, skinless chicken breasts, about 5 oz each, between 2 sheets of lightly oiled plastic wrap and bash with a rolling pin until half their original thickness. Beat 1 egg with 1 teaspoon Dijon mustard. Place 2 cups fresh white bread crumbs in a separate bowl. Dip each chicken breast into the egg mixture and then coat in bread crumbs. Cook under a preheated broiler for 4 minutes on each side until crisp and brown. Meanwhile, stir 1 tablespoon chopped tarragon and 1 teaspoon lemon juice into 4 tablespoons mayonnaise. Serve on the burgers in toasted buns, with salad leaves.

Fried Chicken with Tarragon and Sunblush Tomatoes

Split 4 boneless, skinless chicken breasts, about 5 oz each, in half along their length without cutting all the way through, to produce "pockets." Fill each with 4 sunblush tomatoes and 1 large tarragon sprig and secure with butcher's twine or a wooden toothpick. Heat 2 tablespoons olive oil in a large, heavy skillet and cook the chicken breasts over medium-high heat for 5 minutes on each side. Pour in 1¼ cups chicken stock and bring to a boil. Reduce the heat, cover, and simmer for 10 minutes. Meanwhile, beat 1 egg with 2 teaspoons Dijon mustard. Very slowly whisk in ¾ cup vegetable oil until thick and creamy. Stir in 2 tablespoons chopped tarragon and season. Serve the hot chicken breasts on warmed serving plates with the sauce spooned over.

30 Sausage, Rosemary, and Mixed Bean Hotpot

Serves 4

1 tablespoon olive oil

12 good-quality sausages

1 red onion, sliced

2 Romero red sweet peppers, cored, seeded, and cut into chunks

1 tablespoon rosemary leaves

13 oz can adzuki beans (or any other canned bean), drained and rinsed

13 oz can lima beans, drained and rinsed

13 oz can cherry tomatoes

2/3 cup beef stock

warm crusty whole-wheat bread, to serve (optional)

- Heat the oil in a large, heavy skillet and cook the sausages over medium heat, turning frequently, for 10 minutes until browned all over and cooked through. Remove with a slotted spoon. Pour off most of the oil from the pan and discard, leaving about 1 tablespoon. Add the onion and red peppers to the pan and cook, stirring frequently, for 3–4 minutes until softened. Add the rosemary leaves and cook for 1 minute more.

- Add the drained beans, tomatoes, and stock and bring to a boil. Return the sausages to the pan, reduce the heat to a simmer, and cook for 10 minutes until the beans and sausages are piping hot.

- Serve ladled into warmed serving bowls, with warm crusty whole-wheat bread, if desired.

---

10 Chili and Black-Eyed Pea Hotpot

Heat 1 tablespoon olive oil in a large, heavy saucepan and cook 2 chopped red onions, 1 seeded and finely chopped green chili and 1 teaspoon peeled and finely chopped fresh ginger root over medium heat, stirring occasionally, for 5 minutes. Add 1 teaspoon harissa paste and ⅔ cup pitted and chopped apricots and mix well. Stir in 2 x 13 oz cans cherry tomatoes and a drained 13 oz can black-eyed peas and heat through, stirring occasionally, for 5 minutes. Season with salt and pepper, and serve with prepared couscous and spoonfuls of thick yogurt stirred through with chopped fresh cilantro.

20 Chorizo, Chicken, and Chickpea Hotpot

Heat 1 tablespoon vegetable oil in a large saucepan and cook 3 thinly sliced boneless, skinless chicken breasts, about 5 oz each, 1 chopped onion, and 1 chopped garlic clove over medium heat, stirring frequently, for 5 minutes. Skin and thickly slice 7 oz chorizo sausage and cook with the chicken, stirring, for 2 minutes. Add 2 x 13 oz cans chopped tomatoes, a drained 13 oz can chickpeas, and 1 teaspoon each ground cumin and smoked paprika. Simmer for 10 minutes, season, and add chopped parsley. Serve with wild rice.

Mango and Spinach Salad with Warm Peanut Chicken

Serves 4

2 tablespoons sesame oil

2 boneless, skinless chicken breasts, about 6 oz each, thinly sliced

3 cups spinach and watercress salad

1 large ripe mango, pitted, peeled, and sliced

4 tablespoons crunchy peanut butter

5 tablespoons coconut milk

2 tablespoons sweet chili sauce

4 tablespoons water

- Heat 1 tablespoon of the sesame oil in a large, heavy skillet and cook the sliced chicken over high heat, stirring frequently, for 5–6 minutes until browned and cooked through.

- Meanwhile, place the spinach and watercress salad with the mango in a large serving bowl, drizzle with the remaining sesame oil, and toss to mix.

- Add the remaining ingredients to the chicken in the pan and cook, stirring, for 1 minute. Toss into the salad and serve while still warm.

 ## Chicken and Mango Kebabs

Cut 3 boneless, skinless chicken breasts, about 6 oz each, into cubes and place in a bowl with 4 tablespoons dark soy sauce, a ½ inch piece of fresh ginger root, peeled and chopped, and ½ teaspoon Chinese 5-spice powder. Toss well to coat, cover, and allow to marinate for 5 minutes. Meanwhile, pit, peel, and cut 1 mango into large chunks. Toss in a bowl with 1 tablespoon sesame oil and 2 tablespoons chopped fresh cilantro. Thread the chicken and mango evenly onto 8 metal skewers. Cook the kebabs under a preheated high broiler for 8–10 minutes, turning occasionally, until browned and cooked through.

 ## Chicken Stir-Fry with Mango and Peanut Sauce

Heat 1 tablespoon vegetable oil in a large wok or heavy skillet and cook 4 boneless, skinless chicken breasts, about 5 oz each, cut into chunky cubes, over medium-high heat, stirring frequently, for 8–10 minutes until browned and cooked through. Add 2 large carrots, peeled and cut into thick batons, and stir-fry for 5 minutes until softened. Add 1 bunch of trimmed and chopped scallions and 2 cups sugar snap peas and stir-fry for an additional 2 minutes, then add ½ pitted mango, peeled and cut into thin slices. Cook, tossing, for 1 minute. Remove from the heat.

Blend 3 tablespoons crunchy peanut butter with 2 tablespoons dark soy sauce and ⅔ cup boiling water until smooth. Pour into the stir-fry, return to the heat, and cook for 2 minutes, gently tossing to avoid breaking up the mango.

30 Beef Tenderloin with Mustard Crust and Oven Fries

Serves 4

2 tablespoons butter

1 lb whole beef tenderloin

3 tablespoons whole grain mustard

1 tablespoon Dijon mustard

3 tablespoons thyme leaves

2 tablespoons chopped parsley

salad, to serve (optional)

For the fries

4 baking potatoes, scrubbed and cut into wedges

2 tablespoons olive oil

½ teaspoon sea salt flakes

½ teaspoon English powdered mustard

3 tablespoons chopped parsley

- For the fries, spread the potato wedges out in a large roasting pan and drizzle with the oil. Toss well to lightly coat the potatoes in the oil, then sprinkle with the salt and powdered mustard and toss again. Place in a preheated oven, 425°F, for 20 minutes.

- Meanwhile, melt the butter in a large, heavy skillet and cook the beef briefly over high heat, turning frequently, until browned all over and sealed. Transfer to a work surface. Mix the mustards and herbs together and spread over the beef. Place the beef in the roasting pan with the potatoes if there is room, or in a separate roasting pan, and cook in the oven for 15 minutes until cooked through but still pink in the center.

- Slice the beef into thick or thin slices and serve with the fries tossed in the chopped parsley, accompanied by a simple salad, if desired.

 Minute Steaks with Arugula Sauce
In a food processor, whiz together 1¼ cups arugula leaves, reserving a few leaves for garnish, 4 tablespoons hot horseradish sauce, 1 garlic clove, 1 teaspoon Dijon mustard, and ¾ cup half-fat sour cream. Heat 1 tablespoon olive oil in a large skillet and cook 4 thin-cut sirloin steaks, about 5 oz each, over high heat for 1½ minutes on each side. Allow to rest while gently heating through the sauce. Spoon over the steaks, garnish with the reserved arugula and serve with oven fries.

 Pepper and Mustard Steaks with Butternut Fries Place 12 oz ready-prepared butternut squash wedges in a roasting pan and toss in 2 tablespoons olive oil and ½ teaspoon sea salt flakes. Place in a preheated oven, 425°F, for 15–17 minutes until browned and cooked through. Meanwhile, brush 4 sirloin steaks, about 6 oz each, with olive oil, then coat with 3 tablespoons crushed mixed peppercorns mixed with 3 tablespoons Dijon mustard. Cook in a preheated griddle pan over high heat for 6–8 minutes, turning once.

Allow to rest for 5 minutes before serving with the butternut fries, a spoonful of good mayonnaise, and a leafy salad.

3 Chicken and Chorizo Jambalaya with Peppers

Serves 4

¾ cup long-grain rice

1 tablespoon olive oil

8 oz piece of chorizo sausage, cut into chunky slices

1 onion, chopped

12 oz boneless, skinless chicken breasts, cut into chunks

1 red bell pepper, cored, seeded, and cut into chunks

1 green bell pepper, cut into chunks

1 yellow bell pepper, cut into chunks

2 celery sticks, chopped

2 tablespoons cold water

1 tablespoon cornstarch

2½ cups chicken stock

13 oz can chopped tomatoes

salt and pepper

4 tablespoons chopped parsley

- Bring a saucepan of lightly salted water to a boil and cook the rice for 15 minutes until tender, then drain.

- Meanwhile, heat the oil in a large, heavy skillet and cook the chorizo, onion, and chicken over medium heat, stirring occasionally, for 10 minutes until browned and cooked through. Add the peppers and celery and cook, stirring occasionally, for an additional 5 minutes.

- Blend the measurement water with the cornstarch, then stir into the stock, add to the pan with the tomatoes, and bring to a boil. Reduce the heat and simmer for 5 minutes before adding the cooked rice. Season generously with pepper.

- Serve garnished with the parsley, accompanied by crusty bread and salad, if desired.

1 Creole-Style Jambalaya

Heat 1 tablespoon olive oil in a large saucepan and cook 1 chopped onion over medium heat, stirring occasionally, for 5 minutes. Add 7 oz sliced chorizo sausage, 4 cooked skinless chicken breast fillets, about 5 oz each, chunkily shredded, and 1 teaspoon Creole spice mix. Cook for 1 minute, then add 1½ cups ready-made fresh tomato sauce, 6 tablespoons chicken stock, and 4½ cups ready-cooked egg-fried rice. Stir, heat through, season, and serve.

2 Cajun Chicken Jambalaya

Place 4 boneless, skinless chicken breasts, about 5 oz each, in a plastic bag with 1 tablespoon Cajun spice mix and toss until evenly coated. Cook under a preheated high broiler for 6 minutes on each side until cooked through. Meanwhile, heat through 3⅓ cups ready-cooked long-grain rice according to the package instructions and tip into a large bowl. Add 1¼ cups fresh pineapple cubes, ½ cup finely chopped fresh cilantro, 3 chopped scallions, and 1 seeded and finely chopped red chili. Mix well and season. Slice the chicken breasts and serve on the warm rice with a spoonful each of fresh salsa and plain yogurt.

30 One-Pan Chicken with Honeyed Roots and Stuffing

Serves 4

4 boneless, skin-on chicken breasts, about 6 oz each

2 large baking potatoes, peeled and cut into chunks

6 parsnips, peeled and cut into chunks

6 carrots, peeled and cut into chunks

4 tablespoons olive oil

3 oz package stuffing mix (flavor of your choice)

2 leeks, trimmed, cleaned, and cut into chunks

3 tablespoons honey

2 tablespoons chopped flat-leaf parsley

salt and pepper

- Arrange the chicken breasts in a large roasting pan with the potato, parsnip, and carrot chunks. Drizzle with the oil and toss well to coat the chicken and vegetables in the oil. Season with salt and pepper and place in a preheated oven, 425°F, for 20 minutes.

- Meanwhile, make up the stuffing according to the package instructions and shape into 4 balls.

- Add the stuffing balls to the roasting pan with the leeks and return to the oven for 5–6 minutes until the leeks have just softened.

- Remove the stuffing balls from the roasting pan along with the chicken pieces. Add the honey and parsley to the vegetables in the pan and gently toss to coat. Serve the chicken and stuffing with the roasted vegetables.

---

1 Quick Honeyed Chicken and Vegetables with Stuffing

Make up 3½ oz of stuffing mix according to the package instructions and shape into 4 balls. Cook under a preheated high broiler, turning frequently, for 3–4 minutes until browned. Meanwhile, heat 2 tablespoons olive oil in a large skillet and cook 1½ lb frozen Mediterranean vegetables over high heat, stirring frequently, for 5 minutes. Add 4 ready-cooked skinless chicken breast fillets, about 5 oz each, roughly torn, and heat through for 2 minutes. Add 3 tablespoons honey and 2 tablespoons chopped parsley and gently mix together. Serve the chicken and vegetables with the stuffing on the side.

2 Prosciutto-Wrapped Sausages with Vegetables and Stuffing

Wrap 8 chipolata sausages with 1 slice of prosciutto each, arrange in a large baking dish, and bake in a preheated oven, 400°F, for 5 minutes. Add 1½ lb frozen mixed grilled vegetables to the dish, drizzle with olive oil, and bake for 8 minutes. Meanwhile, make up 3½ oz of stuffing mix according to package instructions and form into balls. Add to the dish and bake for 6 minutes. Drizzle the sausages and vegetables with balsamic vinegar and serve.

Mediterranean Vegetable Pan-Fry with Lamb

Serves 4

2 tablespoons olive oil
8 oz lamb neck fillet
1 Spanish onion, cut into wedges
2 large zucchini, trimmed and cut into chunks
2 teaspoons coriander seeds, lightly crushed
½ teaspoon ground cumin
½ teaspoon ground paprika
1 red bell pepper, cut into chunks
1 garlic clove, sliced
13 oz can cherry tomatoes
handful of chopped fresh cilantro leaves
pepper
warm whole-wheat bread, to serve

- Heat the oil in a large, heavy skillet or wok, and cut the lamb into thin slices. Cook the lamb with the onion over high heat, stirring, for 2–3 minutes until the lamb is browned and the onion slightly softened. Add the zucchini and cook, stirring, for 2 minutes until beginning to soften.

- Add the spices and toss well, then add the red pepper and garlic, reduce the heat, and cook over medium heat for 4–5 minutes until all the vegetables are beginning to soften.

- Add the tomatoes, season generously with pepper and bring to a boil. Reduce the heat, cover, and simmer, stirring occasionally, for 5 minutes until the vegetables are tender yet still retaining their shape.

- Stir in the chopped cilantro before serving with warm whole-wheat bread to mop up the juices.

 Vegetable and Lamb Kebabs

Cut 8 oz lamb neck fillet into small chunks, sprinkle with 1 teaspoon each ground cumin and paprika and season with salt and pepper. Thread onto metal skewers with 2 large zucchini, trimmed and cut into chunks, and 1 cup cherry tomatoes. Lightly brush with olive oil and cook under a preheated high broiler for 8 minutes, turning once, until browned and cooked through. Serve with warm pita breads and store-bought tsatziki.

 Mediterranean Vegetable and Lamb Braise Heat 2 tablespoons olive oil in a large, heavy skillet or wok and cook 8 oz thinly sliced lamb neck fillet and 1 large Spanish onion over high heat, stirring, for 2–3 minutes until the lamb is browned and the onion slightly softened. Add 2 large zucchini, trimmed and cut into chunks, and cook, stirring, for 2 minutes. Add 2 teaspoons lightly crushed coriander seeds and ½ teaspoon each cumin and paprika and toss well, then add 1 red, 1 orange bell and 1 green pepper, cored, seeded, and cut into chunks, and 1 sliced garlic clove. Reduce the heat and cook over medium heat for 4–5 minutes until all the vegetables are beginning to soften. Add a 1 cup cherry tomatoes with ⅔ cup rich lamb stock and bring to a boil. Reduce the heat, cover, and simmer, stirring occasionally, for 15 minutes.

Teriyaki Beef Sandwiches with Bean Sprout Salad

Serves 4

12 oz sirloin steak

2 tablespoons dark soy sauce

1 tablespoon vegetable oil

1 teaspoon Chinese 5-spice powder

1 inch piece of fresh ginger root, peeled and grated

1 large ciabatta loaf, cut into 4 chunky pieces

For the salad

1 cup bean sprouts

1 red bell pepper, cored, seeded, and thinly sliced

4 tablespoons chopped fresh cilantro

1 tablespoon sesame oil

6 tablespoons sweet chili sauce

- Using a very sharp knife, slice the steak into thin shavings, slicing from the top down to the base in sideways slices. Mix together the soy sauce, oil, 5-spice powder, and ginger in a bowl. Add the steak and toss well to coat. Cover and allow to marinate for 5 minutes.

- Arrange the bread pieces on a baking sheet and place in a preheated oven, 400°F, for 10 minutes to heat through.

- Meanwhile, place all the ingredients for the salad in a separate bowl and toss well to mix. Heat a large griddle pan or skillet, lift the beef from the marinade, and cook in batches in a single layer over high heat for 1 minute on each side.

- Fill the warm ciabatta with the beef and spoon the bean sprout salad on top.

Quick Steak and Horseradish Cream Sandwiches Season 4 sirloin steaks, about 5 oz each, with salt and pepper and cook in a preheated griddle pan over high heat for 3 minutes on each side. Remove and allow to rest. Mix together 6 tablespoons sour cream, 4 tablespoons horseradish sauce, and the juice of 1 lemon. Season to taste. Slice the steaks into ½ inch slices. Fill 8 split crusty rolls with the steak, add a spoonful of the horseradish mixture to each, and caramelized onions from a jar. Garnish with watercress.

New York Deli Beef Sandwiches Thinly slice 10 oz cooked lean beef. For the slaw, toss together ½ small chopped red cabbage, ½ finely sliced red onion, the juice of ½ lemon, 1 tablespoon olive oil, a handful of chopped parsley, and salt and pepper. For the dressing, whisk together 4 tablespoons each sour cream and tomato ketchup. Butter 8 slices of sourdough bread, turn over and spread each unbuttered side with a heaping tablespoon of the dressing. Top each of 4 bread slices with a slice of Gruyère cheese, divide the slaw and beef slices between them, and add a sprinkling of chopped parsley. Cover with the remaining slices of bread, buttered-side up, and press down firmly. Cook the sandwiches in a preheated griddle pan over high heat until browned on both sides. Serve with cornichons.

1 Special Fried Rice

Serves 4

2 tablespoons sesame oil

2 eggs, beaten

8 bacon slices, snipped into pieces

1 bunch of scallions, trimmed and roughly chopped

4 oz small cooked peeled shrimp

⅔ cup frozen peas

1¾ cups ready-cooked long-grain rice

salt and pepper

- Heat 1 tablespoon of the oil in a large skillet, pour in the eggs in a thin layer, and cook over medium heat for 1–2 minutes until golden and set. Remove and cut into shreds.

- Add the remaining oil to the pan and stir-fry the bacon and scallions over high heat for 2–3 minutes until the bacon is browned and the scallions softened. Add the shrimp and peas and stir-fry for 1 minute more. Add the rice and stir-fry for 2–3 minutes until hot.

- Add the shredded omelet to the rice and heat through for a few seconds. Season with salt and pepper and serve immediately.

---

2 Stir-Fried Beef and Chili Rice

Bring a saucepan of lightly salted water to a boil and cook 1 cup easy-cook long-grain rice for 15 minutes until tender, then drain. Meanwhile, heat 1 tablespoon sesame oil in a large wok or heavy skillet and stir-fry 10 oz thinly sliced rump steak over high heat for 3–4 minutes until browned. Add 1 bunch of chopped scallions and stir-fry for 2 minutes, then add ⅔ cup peas, defrosted if frozen, and stir-fry for an additional 2 minutes until hot. Stir in ½ cup chopped toasted cashew nuts, 6 tablespoons chopped cilantro, and 5 tablespoons sweet chili sauce and stir-fry for 1 minute to heat through. Add the rice and cook, tossing, for another 2 minutes.

3 Vegetable Fried Rice

Bring a large saucepan of lightly salted water to a boil and cook 1 cup easy-cook long-grain rice for 15 minutes until tender, then drain. Meanwhile, heat 3 tablespoons olive oil in a wok or large, heavy skillet and cook 2 finely chopped celery sticks, 1 trimmed, halved, and thinly sliced small zucchini, and 2 peeled and thinly sliced carrots over high heat, stirring occasionally, for 10 minutes until softened. Set aside. Heat 1 tablespoon sesame oil in a separate large, heavy skillet, pour in the eggs in a thin layer, and cook over medium heat for 1–2 minutes until golden and set. Remove and cut into shreds. Add the drained rice and shredded omelet to the vegetables and toss until well mixed and piping hot. Serve with light soy sauce, if desired.

30 Tray-Baked Sausages with Apples and Onions

Serves 4

3 red onions, cut into wedges

3 red apples, cored and cut into 6 wedges

7 oz baby carrots, scrubbed

3 potatoes, peeled and cut into small cubes

4 tablespoons olive oil

12 good-quality pork sausages

2 tablespoons chopped sage leaves

1 tablespoon rosemary leaves

3 tablespoons honey

salt and pepper

- Place the wedges of onion and apple in a large, shallow roasting pan with the carrots and potatoes. Drizzle over the oil, then toss well to lightly coat all the vegetables in the oil. Season generously with salt and pepper. Arrange the sausages in and around the vegetables, sprinkle with the herbs, and toss again.

- Place in a preheated oven, 400°F, for 20–22 minutes until golden and cooked through.

- Remove from the oven and drizzle over the honey. Toss all the vegetables and sausages in the honey and serve.

10 Quick Pork, Apple, and Onion Stir-Fry

Cut 8 oz pork tenderloin into very thin slices. Heat 2 tablespoons olive oil in a large wok or heavy skillet and stir-fry the pork over high heat for 2–3 minutes. Add 2 cored apples and 2 red onions, each cut into slim wedges, and stir-fry for 3–4 minutes until browned and softened. Add 1 tablespoon chopped sage leaves or rosemary and toss to mix. Serve in warm ciabatta with plenty of Dijon mustard.

20 Simple Sausage, Apple, and Onion Stir-Fry

Cook 12 good-quality pork sausages under a preheated high broiler for 10–12 minutes, turning once, until browned and cooked through. Meanwhile, heat 2 tablespoons olive oil in a large wok or heavy skillet and stir-fry 2 cored apples and 2 red onions, each cut into slim wedges, over high heat for 3–4 minutes until browned and softened. Cut 7 oz baby carrots in half lengthwise and add to the pan with 2 tablespoons chopped sage leaves and stir-fry for an additional 3 minutes. Add 6 tablespoons hot beef stock, cover, and cook for 3 minutes. Remove the cooked sausages from the broiler, cut into thick slices, and add to the pan with 3 tablespoons honey. Toss together, then serve with crusty bread.

3 Chicken Thighs with Lemon Sour Cream and Greens

Serves 4

8 boneless chicken thighs
4 tablespoons thyme leaves
1 tablespoon olive oil
finely grated zest and juice of
   1 lemon
1 tablespoon Dijon mustard
2 x 8 oz containers sour cream
4½ cups baby spinach leaves
pepper
cooked rice or creamy mashed
   potato, to serve

- Season the chicken thighs with plenty of pepper and roll in the thyme leaves. Heat the oil in a large, heavy skillet and cook the chicken thighs over medium heat for 20 minutes until cooked through, turning frequently for the first 10 minutes, then covering with a lid for the final 10 minutes.

- Add the lemon zest and juice to the pan and toss with the chicken. Mix the mustard into one of the containers of sour cream and then add both containers of sour cream to the pan with the spinach leaves. Toss and heat for 2–3 minutes until the spinach has wilted and the sauce is hot.

- Serve with rice or creamy mashed potato.

---

1 Watercress Chicken with Capers, Garlic, and Lemon

Roughly chop 2 cups watercress, ½ garlic clove, and 1 tablespoon capers. Mix with the finely grated zest of 1 lemon and season with salt and pepper. Place on a plate and roll 12 oz mini chicken breast fillets in the watercress mixture until each is evenly coated. Heat ½ tablespoon olive oil in a large skillet, add the chicken and any remaining watercress mixture, and cook over medium heat for 3–4 minutes on each side until cooked through. Serve with a couscous salad.

2 Chicken Tagliatelle with Lemon Sour Cream

Bring a large saucepan of lightly salted water to a boil and cook 12 oz dried tagliatelle for 8–10 minutes until just tender. Drain and keep warm. Heat 1 tablespoon olive oil in a large, heavy skillet and cook 4 thinly sliced boneless, skinless chicken breasts, about 5 oz each, over medium-high heat, stirring frequently, for 4–5 minutes until browned and cooked through. Add 1 cup frozen petit pois and heat gently for 2 minutes. Stir in 6 tablespoons lemon juice, 6 tablespoons sour cream, and a handful of torn basil. Add the cooked pasta, season with salt and pepper, and continue to heat gently while carefully tossing. Serve immediately with plenty of salad leaves.

3⊙ Bacon, Onion, and Egg Pan-Cooked Tart

Serves 4

1 lb potatoes, peeled, and thickly sliced

2 tablespoons olive oil

8 oz Canadian bacon, roughly chopped

1 large onion, sliced

1 cup tub ricotta cheese

2 eggs

4 tablespoons chopped parsley

2½ cups chicken stock

salt and pepper

salad, to serve (optional)

- Bring a large saucepan of lightly salted water to a boil and cook the potatoes for 10 minutes.

- Meanwhile, heat the oil in a large, heavy skillet and cook the bacon and onion over medium heat, stirring frequently, for 5 minutes until the bacon has browned and the onion softened.

- Drain the potatoes well, then add to the skillet and cook, stirring frequently without worrying if the potatoes break up, for 2 minutes.

- Dot spoonfuls of the ricotta over the potato mixture. Beat the eggs and parsley into the stock in a bowl, season with pepper, and pour over the potato mixture. Cook gently for 10 minutes, then cook under a preheated high broiler for an additional 2–3 minutes until golden and set.

- Serve spooned onto warmed serving plates, with a simple salad, if desired.

 Chorizo, Spinach, and Onion Omelet

Tip 8 cups spinach leaves into a colander and slowly pour a kettleful of boiling water over until wilted. Cool under cold running water, then squeeze out all the liquid. Heat 3 tablespoons olive oil in a large skillet and cook 1 finely chopped onion and 4 oz ready-sliced chorizo over medium heat, stirring, for 5 minutes. Beat 6 large eggs in a bowl, season, and stir in the spinach. Pour over the chorizo mixture, cook for 4 minutes, then cook under a high broiler for 1 minute to set the top.

 Bacon and Onion Tortilla Thickly slice a 1 lb 2 oz drained can new potatoes. Heat 2 tablespoons olive oil in a large, heavy skillet and cook 8 oz roughly chopped Canadian bacon and 1 sliced onion over medium heat, stirring frequently, for 5 minutes. Add the potatoes and cook, stirring frequently without worrying if the potatoes break up, for 2 minutes. Beat 6 eggs in a bowl, season, and stir in 4 tablespoons chopped parsley. Pour over the bacon and potato mixture and cook gently for 10 minutes.

Grate 1 oz Manchego cheese over the top of the tortilla and cook under a preheated high broiler for an additional 2–3 minutes until lightly browned and set.

Apricot-Glazed Ham Steaks with Paprika Potatoes

Serves 4

1 lb potatoes, peeled and cut into cubes

4 lean ham steaks, about 4 oz each

3 tablespoons vegetable oil

1 onion, roughly chopped

13 oz can apricots in fruit juice, drained and juice reserved

1 teaspoon ground cinnamon

2 teaspoons ground paprika

3 tablespoons chopped parsley

salt and pepper

- Bring a large saucepan of lightly salted water to a boil and cook the potatoes for 10 minutes. Drain.

- Meanwhile, cook the ham under a preheated high broiler for 5–6 minutes on each side until cooked through.

- While the potatoes and ham are cooking, heat 1 tablespoon of the oil in a large, heavy saucepan and cook the onion over medium heat, stirring frequently, for 3–4 minutes until softened. Add the apricot juice and cinnamon and cook over high heat for 3 minutes to reduce the liquid by half. Remove from the heat and add the apricots, then pour all the mixture into a food processor and whiz to a thick, textured sauce. Return to the saucepan and heat through gently while finishing the potatoes.

- Heat the remaining oil in a large, heavy skillet and cook the drained potatoes over a high heat, stirring frequently, for 5 minutes until golden and crisp. Sprinkle over the paprika, season with pepper, and toss in the parsley.

- Spoon the sauce over the ham to serve, accompanied by the paprika potatoes.

 Spiced Apricot-Glazed Ham

Warm 2 tablespoons apricot jelly in a small saucepan, then stir in ½ teaspoon ground cumin and season with pepper. Cook 4 lean ham steaks, about 4 oz each, under a preheated high broiler, brushing frequently with the glaze, for 5–6 minutes on each side until cooked through. Serve with a container of ready-prepared Moroccan couscous.

 Glazed Ham with Minted Bulghur Wheat Salad Bring a saucepan of water to a boil, add ¾ cup bulghur wheat and simmer for 8 minutes. Add 1 cup frozen peas and 2 trimmed, washed, and thinly sliced leeks and simmer for an additional 3 minutes. Meanwhile, for the glaze, simmer the juice of 1 orange, 2 tablespoons honey, and 2 teaspoons each Worcestershire sauce and Dijon mustard in a small saucepan for 2 minutes. Cook 4 lean ham steaks, about 4 oz each, under a preheated high broiler, brushing frequently with the glaze, for 5–6 minutes on each side until cooked through. Meanwhile, drain the bulghur wheat and vegetables, season, and stir in 2 tablespoons mint sauce. Cut each ham steak in half and serve on a bed of the warm bulghur salad.

30 Coq au Vin-Style Chicken Breasts

Serves 4

2 tablespoons all-purpose flour
4 boneless, skinless chicken
   breasts, about 5 oz each
2 tablespoons olive oil
4 oz smoked pancetta, chopped
2 large red onions, cut into wedges
1 garlic clove, sliced
1 tablespoon rosemary leaves
10 oz brown mushrooms, kept
   whole and stalks trimmed
1¼ cups chicken stock
1¼ cups red wine
salt and pepper

To serve (optional)

crusty bread
cooked green beans

- Place the flour on a plate and season well with salt and pepper. Roll the chicken breasts in the seasoned flour to lightly coat.

- Heat 1 tablespoon of the oil in a large, deep heavy skillet and cook the pancetta and onions over medium-high heat, stirring frequently, for 4–5 minutes until the pancetta is cooked and the onions softened. Add the garlic, rosemary, and mushrooms and cook, stirring, for an additional 2 minutes. Remove the ingredients with a slotted spoon.

- Add the remaining tablespoon of oil to the pan and cook the chicken over medium-high heat, turning occasionally, for 10 minutes until well browned. Add the stock and wine and bring to a boil. Return the pancetta, onion, and mushroom mixture to the pan, then reduce the heat, cover, and cook for 7 minutes until the chicken is cooked through and tender. Remove the lid and cook for an additional 3 minutes. Serve with crusty bread and cooked green beans, if desired.

10 Coq au Pasta

Bring a large pan of salted water to a boil and cook 7 oz dried farfalle for 8–10 minutes or until just tender, then drain. Meanwhile, heat 1 tablespoon olive oil in a large skillet and cook 4 thinly sliced boneless chicken breasts, about 5 oz each, with 4 oz smoked pancetta, chopped, and 1 thinly sliced red onion over high heat, stirring, for 6–7 minutes until the chicken is cooked. Stir in ¾ cup sour cream and 1 table-spoon whole grain mustard, add the drained pasta and toss well.

20 Quick Coq au Vin

Slice 4 boneless, skinless chicken breasts, about 5 oz each, into thin strips and toss in 2 tablespoons all-purpose flour seasoned with salt and pepper. Heat 2 tablespoons olive oil in a large skillet and cook the chicken strips, 4 oz smoked pancetta, chopped, 2 large chopped red onions, 1 sliced garlic clove, 1 tablespoon thyme leaves, and 10 oz whole small button mushrooms, stalks trimmed, over medium-high heat, stirring frequently, for 10 minutes until the chicken is cooked through and the vegetables are tender. Pour in 1¼ cups each chicken stock and red wine and bring to a boil, then simmer for 5 minutes. Serve with crusty bread.

30 Rustic Lamb and Potato Curry

Serves 4

2 tablespoons vegetable oil

1 large onion, roughly chopped

1¼ lb lean lamb, cut into cubes

1 small green chili, roughly chopped (optional)

4 tablespoons korma curry paste

2 x 13 oz cans chopped tomatoes

1¼ cups lamb or chicken stock

2 unpeeled potatoes, roughly cut into cubes

2 cups fresh cilantro, roughly chopped

2/3 cup plain yogurt

- Heat the oil in a large, heavy skillet and cook the onion and lamb over high heat, stirring frequently, for 5 minutes until the lamb is browned all over and the onion softened.

- Add the chili, if using, and cook, stirring, for 1 minute. Stir in the curry paste and cook, stirring, for an additional 2 minutes. Add the tomatoes, stock, and potatoes and bring to a boil. Reduce the heat, cover, and simmer for 10 minutes, then remove the lid and cook for an additional 10 minutes until the lamb is cooked through and the potatoes are tender.

- Remove from the heat, then sprinkle with the cilantro and spoon in the yogurt, ready to stir in and serve.

 Simple Chicken Curry with Naan

Heat 1 tablespoon vegetable oil in a large, heavy pan and cook 3 thinly sliced boneless, skinless chicken breasts, about 6 oz each, over high heat, stirring, for 3 minutes. Stir in 1¼ cups ready-made korma curry sauce and 1 chopped tomato and bring to a boil. Add 4½ cups baby spinach leaves, then reduce the heat, cover, and simmer for 5 minutes or until the chicken is cooked before serving on lightly toasted naan breads.

 Chicken and Potato Curry

Heat 2 tablespoons vegetable oil in a large, heavy skillet and cook 3 roughly sliced boneless, skinless chicken breasts, about 6 oz each, and 8 thinly sliced new potatoes over high heat, stirring frequently, for 5 minutes. Add 4 tablespoons korma curry paste and cook, stirring, for 1 minute. Stir in a 13 oz can chopped tomatoes and 1¼ cups canned coconut milk. Bring to a boil, then reduce the heat and cook over medium heat, stirring

occasionally, for 10 minutes. Serve sprinkled with chopped fresh cilantro.

Mushroom and Cheese Burgers with Cucumber Salsa

Serves 4

1 lb ground steak
1 teaspoon smoked paprika
4 scallions, thinly sliced
1 egg yolk
1 teaspoon prepared
  English mustard
1 tablespoon olive oil
4 brown mushrooms,
  trimmed and sliced
4 good-quality whole-wheat buns
4 slices of Emmental or Gruyère
  cheese

For the salsa

¼ cucumber, roughly chopped
2 tablespoons chopped fresh
  cilantro
pepper

- Place the ground steak in a bowl with the paprika, scallions, egg yolk, and mustard and mix together with a fork until thoroughly blended. Shape into 4 patties.

- Cook the burgers under a preheated high broiler for 10 minutes, turning once, until well browned and cooked through.

- Meanwhile, heat the oil in a large, heavy skillet and cook the mushrooms over high heat, stirring frequently, for 5 minutes until browned. Make the salsa by simply tossing the cucumber and cilantro together, and season with a little pepper.

- Split each bun and serve a burger in each, topped with a slice of cheese to melt, then the mushrooms and a spoonful of salsa.

 Quick and Healthy Mini Burgers

Mix together 10 oz lean ground beef, 1 cup whole-wheat bread crumbs, 1 cup grated carrot, 1 small grated onion, 1 crushed garlic clove, a handful of chopped parsley, and 2 teaspoons Worcestershire sauce. Shape the mixture into 8 small patties and cook under a preheated medium broiler for 3 minutes on each side until cooked through. Serve in split, toasted whole-wheat mini buns with a spoonful of store-bought fresh tomato salsa.

 Mushroom and Beef Burgers with Tarragon Butter Mix 9 tablespoons very soft butter with 2 tablespoons Dijon mustard, 1 tablespoon roughly chopped tarragon, the juice of ½ lemon, and salt and pepper. Lay 4 large mushrooms in a roasting dish, fill the hollows with the tarragon butter, and drizzle with olive oil. Cover with foil and place in a preheated oven, 400°F, for 20–25 minutes, basting occasionally. Meanwhile, mix together 1 lb ground steak, 2 chopped scallions, 1 egg yolk, and salt and pepper. Shape into 4 patties and cook under a preheated high broiler for 10 minutes, turning once, until well browned and cooked through. Serve each burger in a split whole-wheat bun, topped with a slice of Emmental or Gruyère cheese, along with a mushroom drizzled with tarragon butter. Serve with a green salad, if desired.

30 Spicy Cajun Chicken Quinoa with Dried Apricots

Serves 4

2½ cups chicken stock
½ cup quinoa
⅔ cup ready-to-eat dried apricots, roughly chopped
3 boneless, skinless chicken breasts, about 6 oz each, thinly sliced
2 teaspoons Cajun spice mix
2 tablespoons olive oil
2 red onions, cut into slim wedges
2 bunches of scallions, roughly chopped
6 tablespoons chopped fresh cilantro

To serve

whole milk yogurt
crusty bread (optional)

- Place the stock in a saucepan and bring to a boil, add the quinoa, then simmer for 10 minutes. Stir in the apricots and cook for an additional 5 minutes.

- Meanwhile, toss the chicken with the Cajun spice in a bowl to coat. Heat the oil in a large, heavy skillet and cook the chicken and onion wedges over medium-high heat, stirring frequently, for 10 minutes until the chicken is well browned and cooked through. Add the scallions and cook for 1 minute more.

- Drain the quinoa and apricots, then add to the chicken mixture and toss well to mix. Toss in the chopped cilantro and serve with spoonfuls of whole milk yogurt, with crusty bread, if desired.

 Chicken with Fresh Apricot Lentils
Heat 1 tablespoon olive oil in a large skillet and cook 1 finely chopped red onion over medium heat, stirring frequently, for 5 minutes. Pour in 4 tablespoons red wine vinegar and cook for 30 seconds. Add 3½ cups ready-cooked Puy lentils, 4 fresh pitted apricots cut into chunks, and 4 tablespoons each chopped fresh cilantro and mint. Add 4 cooked chicken breast fillets, about 5 oz each, shredded, and heat through for 1 minute. To serve, stir in 1¼ cups arugula.

 Glazed Chicken with Fresh Apricot Quinoa Bring 2½ cups chicken stock to a boil in a saucepan, add ½ cup quinoa, and simmer for 15 minutes. Meanwhile, mix 3 tablespoons marmalade with 4 teaspoons whole grain mustard. Slice 4 boneless, skinless chicken breasts, about 5 oz each, lay in a roasting pan and brush over half the marmalade glaze. Cook under a preheated high broiler for 4–5 minutes, then turn over, brush with the remaining glaze and cook for an additional 4–5 minutes. Pit and cut 4 fresh apricots into chunks, then toss with 4 chopped scallions, 3 tablespoons white wine vinegar, and 1 teaspoon ground cumin. Drain the cooked quinoa, stir in the apricot mixture, and serve with the chicken, sprinkled with extra chopped scallions.

20 Stir-Fried Duck with Sugar Snaps and Orange Rice

Serves 4

1 cup easy-cook long-grain rice
2 tablespoons sesame oil
1 red onion, cut into slim wedges
4 boneless duck breasts,
  skin on, about 5 oz
  each, thickly sliced
1 bunch of scallions, cut
  into 1 inch lengths
1¾ cups sugar snap peas
finely pared rind and juice of
  1 orange
2 tablespoons dark soy sauce
1 tablespoon light brown sugar
salt

- Bring a large saucepan of lightly salted water to a boil and cook the rice for 15 minutes until tender. Drain and keep warm.

- Meanwhile, heat the oil in a large wok or heavy skillet over medium-high heat and stir-fry the red onion for 5 minutes. Add the duck slices and stir-fry for 5 minutes until the duck is almost cooked. Add the scallions and sugar snap peas and stir-fry over high heat for 2 minutes.

- Add the drained rice to the pan and toss well. Mix together the orange rind and juice, soy sauce, and sugar in a small bowl, then pour over the duck mixture and toss well to distribute the sauce through the dish. Serve immediately in warmed serving bowls.

---

10 Chinese Duck Noodles

Heat 2 tablespoons sesame oil in a large wok or heavy skillet over medium-high heat and stir-fry 4 thickly sliced duck breasts, about 5 oz each, for 5 minutes. Add 1 bunch of scallions, cut into 1 inch lengths, and 1¾ cups sugar snap peas and stir-fry over high heat for 2 minutes. Stir in 10 oz ready-cooked Thai rice noodles and 6 tablespoons hoisin sauce and heat through for 2 minutes.

---

30 Duck Breasts with Orange

Heat 1 tablespoon sesame oil in a large wok or heavy skillet and cook 4 boneless duck breasts, about 5 oz each, skin-side down, over high heat for 5 minutes, then turn over and cook for an additional 2 minutes. Transfer to a shallow roasting pan. Add 3 tablespoons each marmalade and orange juice to the wok or skillet and gently heat for a few seconds, stirring to loosen, then pour over the breasts and place in a preheated oven, 400°F, while you prepare the rice. Bring a large saucepan of lightly salted water to a boil and cook 1 cup easy-cook long-grain rice for 15 minutes until tender, then drain. Heat 2 tablespoons sesame oil in the cleaned wok or skillet, add 1 bunch of scallions, chopped, and 1¾ cups sugar snap peas, and stir-fry over high heat for 2 minutes. Add the rice and toss well. Serve with the duck breasts.

Lamb Fillet with Mushroom and Spinach Sauce

Serves 4

2 tablespoons olive oil

2 lamb neck fillet pieces, about
   8 oz each

For the sauce

1 tablespoon butter

8 oz brown mushrooms, trimmed
   and halved

4 oz button mushrooms, trimmed

1 small onion, finely chopped

½ teaspoon ground paprika

3 tablespoons brandy

1¼ cups light cream

5 cups baby spinach leaves

- Heat 1 tablespoon of the oil in large, heavy skillet and cook the lamb over high heat, turning frequently, for 1–2 minutes until browned and sealed all over. Reduce the heat and allow to cook gently while making the sauce, turning once.

- Melt the butter with the remaining tablespoon of oil in a separate large, heavy skillet frying pan and cook the mushrooms and onion over high heat, stirring frequently, for 5 minutes. Add the paprika and cook, stirring, for 1 minute. Add the brandy and cook for a few seconds until the alcohol has evaporated, then remove from the heat and add the cream and spinach.

- Return the pan to the heat, toss, and cook for 3–4 minutes over gentle heat until the spinach has wilted and the sauce is hot.

- Slice the lamb thickly, arrange on warmed serving plates, and spoon large spoonfuls of the mushroom and spinach sauce over.

 Quick Lamb Steaks with Creamy Mushrooms Cook 4 lamb steaks, about 5 oz each, under a preheated high broiler for 4–5 minutes on each side. Meanwhile, place 3 tablespoons brandy in a saucepan with a drained 10 oz can button mushrooms and heat for around 3 minutes until boiling, then reduce the heat to low, add 1¾ cups light cream and stir until piping hot but not boiling. Spoon the sauce over the lamb steaks and serve.

 Lamb Meatballs with Mushroom and Spinach Sauce Mix together 1 lb finely ground lamb, 2 teaspoons garlic paste, and ½ teaspoon paprika and shape into 12 balls. Heat a large, heavy skillet, add the meatballs, and cook over medium-high heat, turning frequently, while making the mushroom and spinach sauce as above. Serve the meatballs drizzled with the sauce.

30 Smoky Chicken and Shrimp Paella

Serves 4

2 tablespoons olive oil

2 skinless chicken breasts, about
 5 oz each, thinly sliced

1 large Spanish onion, thinly sliced

4 oz chorizo, chopped

1 red bell pepper, chopped

1 green bell pepper, chopped

2 teaspoons smoked paprika

few saffron threads

1¼ cups Arborio risotto rice

3¾ cups hot chicken stock

4 tomatoes, roughly chopped

1 cup green beans, trimmed

⅔ cup frozen peas

7 oz large cooked peeled shrimp

salt and pepper

- Heat the oil in a large, heavy skillet and cook the chicken and onion over medium-high heat, stirring frequently, for 5 minutes until the chicken is well browned and the onion is softened. Add the chorizo and peppers and cook, stirring frequently, for 3 minutes.

- Add the paprika and saffron to the pan and stir well, then add the rice and toss well to coat the grains in the spices. Season with a little salt and pepper. Add the stock and tomatoes and bring to a boil. Reduce the heat, cover, and simmer, stirring occasionally and adding more water or stock if necessary, for 10 minutes until the rice is tender.

- Stir in the beans, peas, and shrimp and cook for an additional 5 minutes. Serve immediately.

 Simple Smoky Chicken and Shrimp Pilaff Heat 2 tablespoons olive oil in a large skillet and cook 2 very thinly sliced skinless chicken breasts, about 5 oz each, 4 oz chopped chorizo sausage, and 1 chopped red bell pepper over medium-high heat, stirring frequently, for 5–6 minutes until the chicken is cooked through. Add 3⅓ cups ready-cooked long-grain rice, 4 chopped fresh tomatoes, and ⅔ cup frozen peas and stir-fry over high heat for 3 minutes until the rice is hot and the tomatoes are pulpy. Serve with chopped parsley.

 Smoky Chicken and Shrimp Risotto Place 1¼ cups Arborio risotto or paella rice in a large, heavy skillet with a few saffron threads, ½ teaspoon salt, and 1 tablespoon olive oil and cook over medium heat, stirring, for 1 minute. Add 5 cups hot rich chicken stock and bring to a boil. Reduce the heat, cover, and simmer for 15 minutes until tender. Meanwhile, in a separate heavy skillet, cook 1 cored, seeded, and chopped red bell pepper, 1 chopped onion, 4 oz chopped chorizo sausage, and 2 sliced boneless, skinless chicken breasts, about 5 oz each, over medium-high heat, stirring frequently, for 10 minutes until the chicken is cooked through. Stir in 1 teaspoon smoked paprika, then toss into the cooked rice with 1¼ cups defrosted frozen peas and 4 oz cooked peeled shrimp. Cook for 5 minutes, season well with pepper, and serve with freshly grated Parmesan cheese, if desired.

Honey-Glazed Pork Chops with Spinach Mash

Serves 4

1 tablespoon honey

1 tablespoon whole grain mustard

4 small pork chops, about 6 oz each

3½ oz package instant mashed potato

3 tablespoons sour cream

3½ tablespoons butter

4¼ cups spinach leaves

pepper

- Mix together the honey and mustard, then brush over the chops. Cook under a preheated medium broiler for 3–4 minutes on each side or until cooked through.

- Meanwhile, make up the instant mash according to the package instructions, season with pepper, and mix in the sour cream. Melt the butter in a large saucepan and cook the spinach over medium heat, stirring, for 2 minutes until just wilted.

- Stir the spinach into the mash and serve with the pork chops.

---

2 Creamy Pork and Mustard with

Instant Mash Heat 2 tablespoons olive oil in a large, heavy skillet and cook 4 thinly sliced pork steaks and 2 red onions, cut into slim wedges, over medium heat, stirring occasionally, for 7–8 minutes until the pork is browned and cooked through and the onion is tender. Add ⅔ cup hard cider, bring to a boil and continue boiling for 2 minutes until the liquid has reduced by half. Add ¾ cup sour cream and 1 tablespoon whole grain mustard and season well with salt and pepper. Heat through for 2–3 minutes, then stir in 3 tablespoons chopped parsley. Serve with instant mash, prepared according to the package instructions.

---

3 Spinach Mash-Topped Pork and

Apple Pie Heat 1 tablespoon vegetable oil in a large, heavy skillet and cook 1 lb ground pork with 1 chopped onion over medium heat, stirring, for 10 minutes until browned and cooked through. Add 1 cup ready-made applesauce and 3 tablespoons chopped sage and cook, stirring occasionally, for an additional 5 minutes. Season well, then transfer to a large, shallow gratin dish. Melt 2 tablespoons butter in a large saucepan and cook 4¼ cups spinach leaves over medium heat, stirring, for 2 minutes until wilted. Stir into 2 x 1 lb containers ready-made fresh mashed potato and spoon over the top of the pork. Place under a preheated broiler for 5 minutes until piping hot and golden.

30 Asian-Style Beef Skewers with Satay Sauce

Serves 4

12 oz rump or sirloin steak
6 tablespoons dark soy sauce
2 tablespoons sesame oil
2 tablespoons rice vinegar or mirin
1 tablespoon dark brown sugar
1 inch piece of fresh ginger root, peeled and finely grated
1 garlic clove, crushed
crudités, such as carrots, sugar snap peas, and cucumber

For the sauce

6 tablespoons crunchy peanut butter
3 tablespoons dark soy sauce
1 small red chili, finely chopped
⅔ cup boiling water

- Cut the steak into long, thin strips. Mix together the soy sauce, oil, vinegar or mirin, sugar, ginger, and garlic in a nonmetallic bowl. Add the steak and toss well to coat. Cover and allow to marinate for 15 minutes.

- Meanwhile, heat all the ingredients for the sauce in a pan over very gentle heat, stirring constantly with a wooden spoon, until smooth and thick. Transfer to a small serving bowl and place on a serving platter with the crudités.

- Thread the beef onto 8 metal skewers, or bamboo skewers presoaked in cold water for 30 minutes, and cook under a preheated high broiler for 2 minutes on each side until browned and just cooked.

- Transfer to the serving platter with the sauce and crudités and serve immediately.

 Asian-Style Teriyaki Beef on Lettuce Platters Slice 12 oz trimmed sirloin steak into thin slices and mix with 2 tablespoons bottled teriyaki marinade in a bowl. In a separate bowl, dice ½ cucumber and mix with 2 tablespoons chopped cilantro, 1 teaspoon dried red pepper flakes, and the juice of 1 lime. Heat 1 teaspoon vegetable oil in a large skillet and cook the steak over high heat for 1 minute on each side. Pile the cucumber mixture into 8 small crisphead lettuce leaves, top with beef, and sprinkle with chopped scallions.

 Asian-Style Turkey Satay Kebabs Thread 8 metal skewers alternately with 1 lb turkey steaks, cut into cubes, 1 red bell pepper, cored, seeded, and cut into chunks, and 1¼ cups fresh pineapple chunks, juice reserved. Mix together ¾ cup coconut cream, ½ cup ready-made satay stir-fry sauce, and the pineapple juice, and drizzle about 2 tablespoons over each kebab. Cook under a preheated high broiler for 2 minutes on each side. Meanwhile, heat through the remaining satay sauce and stir in ½ cup chopped fresh cilantro. Serve the kebabs drizzled with the hot sauce and sprinkled with shredded basil on a bed of cooked egg noodles.

Lamb and Tray-Roasted Vegetables with Chickpeas

Serves 4

1 tablespoon olive oil

8 lamb chops

1 eggplant, trimmed and cut into cubes

1 large red onion, cut into chunks

2 zucchini, trimmed and cut into chunks

1 red bell pepper, cored, seeded, and cut into chunks

1 yellow bell pepper, cored, seeded, and cut into chunks

12 oz tomatoes, cut into quarters

1 teaspoon ground cumin

1 teaspoon ground coriander

13 oz can chickpeas, drained

3 tablespoons pumpkin seeds

- Heat the oil in a large, heavy skillet and cook the lamb chops over high heat for 1 minute on each side until browned and sealed. Transfer to a large roasting pan with a spatula, reserving the cooking juices in the pan, and place in a preheated oven, 425°F, while pan-frying the vegetables.

- Add the eggplant, onion, zucchini, and peppers to the skillet and cook over high heat, stirring frequently, for 5 minutes. Add the tomatoes and cook, stirring, for 2 minutes.

- Transfer all the vegetables to the roasting pan with the lamb, add the spices and chickpeas, and toss to mix. Return to the top shelf of the oven for an additional 10 minutes or until the lamb is cooked through.

- Sprinkle with the pumpkin seeds before serving.

 Moroccan-Style Lamb and Vegetable Stir-Fry Heat 1 tablespoon olive oil in a large, heavy skillet pan and cook 12 oz thinly sliced lamb neck fillet, 1 red and 1 yellow bell pepper, cored, seeded, and cut into chunks, and 2 zucchini, trimmed and cut into chunks, over high heat, stirring frequently, for 8 minutes until the lamb is cooked through. Add a squeeze of garlic paste, 1 teaspoon each ground cumin and coriander, and a 13 oz can chopped tomatoes, stir well, and cook for an additional 2 minutes.

 Pesto Lamb and Vegetable Bake Prepare the recipe as above, but instead of flavoring the lamb and vegetables with cumin and coriander, make your own green pesto instead. In a food processor, whiz together a handful of basil leaves, 3 tablespoons olive oil, the juice of 1 lemon, ¼ cup freshly grated Parmesan cheese, and ½ cup pine nuts until smooth. Toss the pesto into the roasting pan with the lamb, pan-fried vegetables, and chickpeas, and bake as above.

30 Turkey Meatballs in Rich Tomato and Herb Sauce

Serves 4

1 lb ground turkey
1 cup fresh white bread crumbs
4 scallions, thinly sliced
1 tablespoon ground paprika
6 tablespoons chopped parsley
2 tablespoons olive oil
1 onion, finely chopped
13 oz cans chopped tomatoes
3 tablespoons sundried tomato
  paste
2 tablespoons chopped chives
pepper
cooked rice or noodles, or
  mashed potato, to serve

- Place the ground turkey in a bowl with the bread crumbs, scallions, paprika, and 3 tablespoons of the parsley and mix together with a fork until thoroughly blended. Shape into 20–24 balls.

- Heat 1 tablespoon of the oil in a large skillet and cook the meatballs over medium heat for 20 minutes, turning frequently, until browned all over and cooked through.

- Meanwhile, heat the remaining tablespoon of oil in a separate large, heavy skillet and cook the onion over medium-high heat, stirring frequently, for 2–3 minutes until just softened. Add the tomatoes and tomato paste and season generously with pepper. Bring to a boil, stirring constantly, then reduce the heat and simmer for 10 minutes until the sauce has reduced a little and thickened.

- Stir the remaining parsley and the chives into the sauce, then stir in the cooked meatballs. Serve with cooked rice or noodles, or mashed potato.

---

10 Chickpea and Herb Balls

In a food processor, combine ½ cup chopped Parmesan cheese, 1 cup fresh bread crumbs, 1 egg, a drained 13 oz can chickpeas, 2 garlic cloves, 1 teaspoon dried oregano, and a few basil leaves. Shape into 16 balls. Heat 2 tablespoons olive oil in a large skillet and cook the balls, turning frequently, for 5–6 minutes until browned all over. Meanwhile, warm through a 1½ cups ready-made fresh arrabbiata pasta sauce. Serve the balls over cooked pasta, topped with the sauce.

20 Moroccan-Style Meatballs

Heat 1 tablespoon olive oil in a large, heavy skillet and cook 12 oz ready-prepared beef meatballs over medium-high heat, turning frequently, for 10 minutes. Remove from the pan, then add 1 large sliced onion and cook, stirring frequently, for 5 minutes. Add ⅔ cup ready-to-eat dried apricots, chopped, 1 teaspoon ground cinnamon, ½ teaspoon ground cumin, and a 13 oz can chopped tomatoes with garlic. Return the meatballs to the pan and bring to a boil, then simmer for 5 minutes or until cooked through. Serve over prepared plain couscous, sprinkled with chopped fresh cilantro and a handful of toasted slivered almonds.

30 Pork Scallops with Prosciutto

Serves 4

4 pieces pork tenderloin, about
  9 oz each
1 egg, beaten
2 cups fresh white bread crumbs
2 tablespoons chopped parsley
4 tablespoons olive oil
4 thin slices of prosciutto
4 thin slices of Gruyère cheese
pepper

To serve (optional)

green salad
crusty bread

- Place the pork tenderloin between 2 sheets of lightly greased plastic wrap and bash with a rolling pin until half their original thickness and almost doubled in size. Place the beaten egg in a shallow bowl. Mix the bread crumbs with the parsley on a plate and season with pepper.

- Dip the pork scallops into the egg to lightly coat and then lightly coat in the herbed bread crumbs.

- Heat the oil in a large, heavy skillet and cook the pork, in batches if necessary, over high heat for 1–2 minutes on each side until the bread crumbs are pale golden. Transfer the pork to a large baking sheet and arrange a slice of prosciutto on top of each and then a slice of Gruyère.

- Place in a preheated oven, 400°F, for 10 minutes until cooked through and the cheese is melted. Serve with a simple green salad and crusty bread, if desired.

 Sage and Mustard Pork Scallops

Bash 4 pieces pork tenderloin, about 9 oz each, as in the recipe above. Wrap a Canadian bacon slice around each, tucking in 2 sage leaves and securing with a wooden toothpick. Make a dressing by mixing 2 tablespoons olive oil, 1 tablespoon honey, 2 teaspoons each white wine vinegar and whole grain mustard, and 1 teaspoon Worcestershire sauce. Heat 1 tablespoon olive oil in a large skillet and cook the pork over high heat for 3 minutes on each side, basting with the dressing throughout.

 Two-Cheese-Crusted Pork Scallops Bash 4 pieces pork tenderloin, about 9 oz each, as in the recipe above. Season with pepper. Mix together 4 tablespoons fresh white bread crumbs, ¾ cup grated mature cheddar cheese, 2 tablespoons melted butter, and 1 tablespoon snipped chives. Cook the pork under a preheated high broiler for about 3 minutes on one side, then turn over and spread 6 oz soft goat cheese over the uncooked sides. Sprinkle with the bread crumb mixture and return to the broiler for 3–4 minutes until cooked through. Serve immediately, sprinkled with a few extra chives. Serve with buttered green beans.

30 Sticky Ham Steaks with Caramelized Onions

Serves 4

1 tablespoon olive oil
4 lean ham steaks, about 4 oz
   each
1 tablespoon butter
2 onions, sliced
2 teaspoons thyme leaves
4 tablespoons thick-cut
   marmalade
1 tablespoon whole grain mustard
1¼ cups hot chicken stock
instant mashed potato, to serve
   (optional)

- Heat the oil in a large, heavy skillet and cook the ham steaks over high heat for 5 minutes, turning once. Remove with a slotted spoon and keep warm.

- Melt the butter in the pan, add the onions and thyme leaves, and cook over low heat, stirring occasionally, for 15 minutes until softened and beginning to caramelize. Stir in the marmalade, mustard, and stock and bring to a boil, then gently simmer for 2–3 minutes until beginning to thicken.

- Return the warm steaks to the pan and simmer for an additional 3 minutes until the sauce is thick and sticky and the steaks are piping hot. Serve with instant mash, if desired.

---

10 Sticky Bacon and Onion Pan-Fry

Heat 1 tablespoon olive oil in a large, heavy skillet and cook 12 Canadian bacon slices, cut into big pieces, and 2 thinly sliced onions over high heat, stirring frequently, for 4 minutes until the bacon is browned and cooked. Meanwhile, mix together 3 tablespoons each marmalade and orange juice and 1 teaspoon each whole grain mustard and thyme leaves. Add to the pan and cook, stirring, for 2 minutes until piping hot. Serve as a baked potato filling, cooking the potatoes in a microwave oven, or on thick slices of buttered toast, topped with grated cheese, if desired.

20 Sticky Glazed Ham Strip Stir-Fry

Cut 4 lean ham steaks, about 4 oz each, into thin strips. Melt 1 tablespoon butter with 1 tablespoon olive oil in a large, heavy skillet and cook the ham strips with 2 sliced onions, 1 cored, seeded, and sliced orange bell pepper, and 2 teaspoons thyme leaves over high heat, stirring frequently, for 8–10 minutes until browned and cooked through. Add 1 cup snow peas and cook, stirring frequently, for an additional 2 minutes. Mix together 2 tablespoons each marmalade and orange juice and 1 tablespoon dark soy sauce, pour into the pan, and toss for 1–2 minutes until the glaze is piping hot and lightly covering all the ingredients. Serve with ready-cooked long-grain rice, heated through according to the package instructions, if desired.

 # Creamy Coconut Beef Rendang

Serves 4

1¼ cups Thai jasmine rice
(optional)

2 tablespoons vegetable oil

1 tablespoon peeled and finely
chopped fresh ginger root

1 bird's eye chili, thinly sliced

1 garlic clove, thinly sliced

1 lemon grass stalk, thinly sliced

1 lb frying steak, cut into strips

½ teaspoon ground cinnamon

pinch of ground turmeric

juice of 1 lime

1¾ cups canned reduced-fat
coconut milk

4 tablespoons chopped fresh
cilantro

- Cook the rice, if using, according to the package instructions.

- Meanwhile, heat the oil in a large, heavy skillet or wok and cook the ginger, chili, garlic, and lemon grass over medium heat, stirring frequently, for 1–2 minutes until softened but not browned. Add the beef, increase the heat to high, and stir-fry for 5 minutes until browned and cooked through.

- Stir in the cinnamon and turmeric and cook, stirring, for a few seconds before adding the lime juice and coconut milk. Gently heat, stirring, for 2–3 minutes until the sauce is hot.

- Serve immediately with the cooked jasmine rice, if using, and sprinkle with the chopped cilantro.

---

10 Speedy Thai-Style Beef and Coconut Skewers Cut 1 lb tenderloin steak into chunks. Thread onto 8 metal skewers alternately with 2 red bell peppers, cored, seeded, and cut into chunky pieces. Mix 4 tablespoons Thai red curry paste with ¾ cup coconut cream and spoon over the skewers. Cook under a preheated high broiler for 3–4 minutes on each side or until cooked through. Serve with warm pita bread.

30 Coconut and Lemon Grass Beef Skewers Cut 1 lb tenderloin steak into chunks. Lightly pound the beef chunks and the base of 4 lemon grass stalks with the end of a rolling pin. Pierce each piece of meat top and bottom with a knife, then thread a lemon grass stalk through, thin end first, to form skewers. Mix together 4 tablespoons Thai red or green curry paste and ¾ cup coconut cream and spoon over the meat. Set aside. Meanwhile, cook 1¼ cups Thai fragrant rice according to the package instructions, adding 10 dried kaffir lime leaves at the start of cooking. Cook the skewers under a preheated high broiler for 3–4 minutes on each side. Serve with the rice and stir-fried bok choy.

Fruity Stuffed Pork Tenderloin with Rosemary

Serves 4

2 pork tenderloins, about 8–10 oz each
3 tablespoons roughly chopped rosemary leaves
3 tablespoons olive oil
1 onion, finely chopped
2 fresh peaches, pitted and roughly chopped
½ teaspoon ground coriander
pinch of ground cumin
pepper

- Lay the pork tenderloins on a cutting board and make a cut across the meat lengthwise through the center, about ¾ inch away from the other side, and open out. Sprinkle the rosemary leaves over both the inside and then the outside of the meat pieces and season generously with pepper.

- Heat 2 tablespoons of the oil in a large skillet and cook the onion over medium heat, stirring, for 4 minutes until softened. Add the peaches and spices and cook for 1 minute.

- Spoon half the peach mixture down the center of one of the tenderloins and the remaining mixture down the center of the other. Gently press the meat back together and tie with butcher's twine in several places to hold the stuffing in place.

- Heat the remaining tablespoon of oil in the cleaned skillet and cook the pork over gentle heat, turning frequently, for 20 minutes, covering the pan for the final 5–10 minutes of the cooking time, until cooked through and tender.

Fruity Pork Steak Pan-Fry

Mix the juice of 3 oranges with 1 tablespoon chopped rosemary leaves and 2 crushed garlic cloves in a small bowl. Take 4 thin-cut pork loin steaks, about 5 oz each, and smear all over with the orange mixture. Heat 1 tablespoon olive oil in a large skillet and cook the steaks over high heat for about 3 minutes on each side until cooked through. Serve with prepared plain couscous and lemon wedges, and any juices from the pan.

Fruity and Sticky Broiled Pork Steaks

Brush 4 pork steaks, about 5 oz each, with a little olive oil, season with salt and pepper, and place on a broiler pan. Pit and quarter 2 ripe peaches and arrange around the pork. Dot with butter and sprinkle with a pinch of dried red pepper flakes and 2 teaspoons brown sugar. Cook under a preheated medium broiler for 15 minutes, turning halfway through, until the pork steaks are browned and cooked through and the peaches are soft and sticky. Drizzle any sticky juices in the broiler pan over the pork.

30 Poached Chicken with Thai Red Curry Sauce

Serves 4

2½ cups chicken stock
1 bunch of scallions, roughly
  chopped
1 inch piece of fresh ginger root,
  peeled and roughly chopped
handful of fresh cilantro stalks
1 lemon grass stalk, chopped
1 lb boneless, skinless chicken
  breast, cut into cubes
cooked Thai jasmine rice, to serve

For the sauce

1 tablespoon vegetable oil
2 tablespoons Thai red curry paste
¾ cup coconut cream
4 tablespoons chopped cilantro
2 teaspoons Thai fish sauce

- Place the stock, 2 of the scallions, roughly chopped, the ginger, cilantro stalks, and lemon grass in a saucepan and bring to a boil. Reduce the heat to a simmer and add the chicken cubes. Poach the chicken for 10 minutes. Remove the chicken with a slotted spoon and set aside (don't worry if some of the flavorings come with the chicken). Strain the stock and reserve ⅔ cup in a measuring cup.

- For the sauce, heat the oil in a heavy saucepan and cook the remaining scallions, finely chopped, over medium-high heat, stirring, for 1 minute. Add the curry paste and cook, stirring, for 1 minute. Add the coconut cream and mix well, then stir in the reserved stock. Add the cilantro and fish sauce, return the chicken to the pan, and stir well. Heat over gentle heat for 5 minutes until the sauce has thickened a little and the chicken is piping hot.

- Serve spooned over cooked Thai jasmine rice in warmed serving bowls.

---

10 Quick Thai Red Curry with Coconut Chicken

Heat a large wok or skillet and stir-fry 2 tablespoons Thai red curry paste with a splash of coconut milk from a 13 oz can over medium heat for 1 minute. Pour in the remaining coconut milk and bring up to a simmer. Add 4 sliced skinless chicken breasts, about 5 oz each, and 1 cup green beans, and simmer for 5 minutes. Add ½ cup cherry tomatoes and cook for an additional 3 minutes. Serve with cooked Thai jasmine rice.

20 Salmon Thai Red Curry

Rinse ½ cup green lentils, then place in a saucepan, cover generously with boiling water, and simmer for 15 minutes. Meanwhile, heat 1 tablespoon vegetable oil in a large, heavy skillet and cook 1 cored, seeded, and sliced red bell pepper over medium-high heat, stirring frequently, for 2 minutes. Add 4 skinless salmon fillets, about 5 oz each, cut into cubes, and cook, stirring gently, for 1 minute. Stir in 6 tablespoons Thai red curry paste, a 13 oz can coconut milk, and 2 cups snow peas, and simmer for 4–5 minutes. Drain the lentils and add to the salmon, then sprinkle with chopped fresh cilantro. Serve with steamed rice.

QuickCook
Fab Fish

Recipes listed by cooking time

10

Parmesan-Crusted Haddock with Tomato Avocado Salsa

Serves 4

4 haddock fillets, about 6 oz each,
  skin removed
juice of ½ lemon
½ cup freshly grated Parmesan
  cheese
1 teaspoon freshly ground black
  pepper
arugula salad, to serve

For the salsa

1 avocado, pitted, peeled, and
  roughly chopped
3 vine-ripened tomatoes, roughly
  chopped
4 tablespoons chopped parsley
2 tablespoons olive oil
pepper

- Place the haddock fillets on a plate and drizzle with the lemon juice. Mix the Parmesan with the pepper on a separate plate. Press the haddock fillets into the Parmesan mixture on one side only to coat.

- Lay the haddock, Parmesan-side up, on a broiler rack lined with foil and cook under a preheated high broiler for 5–6 minutes until golden and cooked through.

- Meanwhile, mix together all the ingredients for the salsa in a bowl and season with plenty of pepper.

- Serve the hot haddock fillets with the salsa spooned over, with a simple arugula salad and lemon wedges, if desired.

 Tapenade-Crusted Haddock with Tomato Olive Salsa Lay 4 haddock fillets, about 6 oz each, skin removed, on a foil-lined broiler rack and spread each with 1 tablespoon store-bought black olive tapenade. Cook under a preheated broiler for 5–6 minutes until cooked through. Meanwhile, mix together 1 pitted, peeled, and roughly chopped avocado, 3 roughly chopped vine-ripened tomatoes, 4 tablespoons chopped basil, a handful of pitted black olives, and 2 tablespoons olive oil in a bowl. Season with pepper and serve with the haddock fillets.

 Parmesan-Crusted Haddock with Vegetable Stew Heat 2 tablespoons olive oil in a heavy saucepan and cook 1 teaspoon chopped rosemary leaves and 1 bay leaf over medium heat for 1 minute. Finely chop 1 onion, 1 large garlic clove, 1 celery stick, 1 carrot, and 4 small trimmed zucchini, add to the pan and cook, stirring occasionally, for 7–8 minutes until just tender. Add a drained 13 oz can chickpeas and ⅔ cup fish stock and simmer for 10 minutes. Meanwhile, prepare and cook 4 haddock fillets, about 6 oz each, skin removed, as above. Stir the juice of ½ lemon and 2 tablespoons chopped parsley into the vegetables and serve the haddock on a bed of the stew.

Salmon with Green Vegetables

Serves 4

1 tablespoon olive oil

1 leek, trimmed, cleaned, and thinly sliced

1¼ cups fish stock

¾ cup sour cream

¾ cup frozen peas

¾ cup frozen soy (edamame) or fava beans

4 chunky skinless salmon fillets, about 5 oz each

2 tablespoons snipped chives

instant mashed potato, to serve

pepper

- Heat the oil in a large, heavy skillet and cook the leek over medium heat, stirring frequently, for 3 minutes until softened. Add the fish stock, bring to a boil, and continue boiling for 2 minutes until reduced a little. Add the sour cream and stir well to mix. Add the peas, soy (edamame) or fava beans, and salmon and return to a boil.

- Reduce the heat, cover, and simmer for 10 minutes until the fish is opaque and cooked through and the peas and beans are piping hot.

- Sprinkle with the chives and serve spooned over creamy instant mash with butter and a good gzesting of pepper.

Creamy Salmon and Green Vegetable Pasta Bring a large saucepan of lightly salted water to a boil and cook 1 lb fresh tagliatelle for 3–4 minutes or until just tender, then drain. Meanwhile, melt 1 tablespoon butter in a heavy skillet and cook 2 skinless salmon fillets, about 5 oz each, cut into small cubes, and ⅓ cup frozen peas over medium heat, stirring gently, for 3 minutes. Add 16 thin asparagus spears, trimmed and chopped into 1½ inch pieces, pour in 5 tablespoons fish stock and 1¼ cups light cream, and cook gently for an additional 5 minutes. Toss the drained pasta into the salmon and cream and serve garnished with torn basil or parsley leaves.

Salmon and Green Vegetable Quiche In a large, store-bought ready-made savory shortcrust pastry shell, arrange 1 chopped leek, ¼ cup frozen fava beans, ⅓ cup frozen peas, 2 tablespoons chopped chives, and 2 skinless salmon fillets, about 5 oz each, cut into ¾ inch cubes. Mix together 2 large eggs, 1 egg yolk, 1¼ cups heavy cream, a pinch of cayenne pepper, and freshly grated nutmeg and pour over the salmon and vegetables. Transfer to a baking sheet and bake in a preheated oven, 350°F, for 25 minutes until the egg mixture is set and browned.

Rich Tomato and Fish Stew

Serves 4

1 tablespoon olive oil
1 onion, thinly sliced
1 garlic clove, chopped
2 tomatoes, roughly chopped
13 oz can chopped tomatoes
4 tablespoons sundried tomato
  paste
⅔ cup white wine
12 oz mixed skinless fish fillets, cut
  into chunks
6 oz raw peeled shrimp
5 tablespoons chopped thyme
½ cup pitted black olives
pepper
warm crusty bread, to serve

- Heat the oil in a large, heavy saucepan and cook the onion and garlic over medium heat, stirring frequently, for 3–4 minutes until softened. Add the fresh tomatoes and cook, stirring, for 2–3 minutes, then add the canned tomatoes, tomato paste and wine. Bring to a boil and cook over high heat for 5 minutes until the sauce is thick.

- Stir the fish chunks and shrimp into the tomato mixture, then reduce the heat, cover, and simmer for 7–8 minutes until the fish is opaque and cooked through and the shrimp have turned pink. Stir through the thyme and black olives and season with pepper to taste.

- Serve in warmed serving bowls with warm crusty bread to mop up the juices.

---

10 Instant Fish Stew

Heat 1 tablespoon olive oil in a heavy saucepan and cook 1 finely chopped onion with a squeeze of garlic paste over medium heat, stirring, for 3 minutes. Add a 13 oz can lobster bisque, a 7 oz can chopped tomatoes, 6 oz mixed skinless fish fillets, cut into chunks, and 6 oz cooked peeled shrimp and cook over high heat for 7 minutes until the seafood is cooked through. Serve with crusty bread.

30 Rich Fish Curry

Mix together 1 teaspoon each fennel, cumin and cilantro seeds, and ground cinnamon, ½ teaspoon each fenugreek seeds and black peppercorns, and 1 clove. Spread out on a baking sheet and toast under a preheated high broiler for 3–4 minutes. Heat 1 tablespoon olive oil in a large, heavy saucepan and cook 1 thinly sliced onion and 1 chopped garlic clove over medium heat, stirring frequently, for 3–4 minutes until softened. Add 2 roughly chopped tomatoes and cook, stirring, for 2–3 minutes. Add a 13 oz can chopped tomatoes, the toasted spices, and ⅔ cup fish stock. Bring to a boil and then simmer briskly, uncovered, for 10 minutes. Stir in 6 oz mixed skinless fish fillets, cut into chunks, and 6 oz cooked peeled shrimp. Cover and simmer for 7–8 minutes until the seafood is cooked through. Stir through 2 large handfuls of torn fresh cilantro and serve.

Crispy Cod Goujons with Lime and Caper Mayonnaise

Serves 4

¾ cup all-purpose flour

1 lb skinless cod fillet, cut into strips

5 cups white bread crumbs

finely grated zest of 2 limes

1 teaspoon black peppercorns, crushed

2 eggs

⅔ cup vegetable oil

salt and pepper

For the mayonnaise

¾ cup sour cream

6 tablespoons mayonnaise

grated zest and juice of 1 lime

2 tablespoons capers, roughly chopped

3 tablespoons chopped parsley

1 tablespoon chopped chives

- Place the flour on a plate and season generously with salt and pepper. Toss the fish strips in the seasoned flour and set aside. Place the bread crumbs on a separate plate and toss with the lime zest and crushed peppercorns. Beat the eggs thoroughly in a shallow bowl.

- Heat the oil in a large, heavy skillet. Meanwhile, dip each floured goujon in the egg and then in the bread crumbs, working swiftly until they are all crumbed. Cook in 2 batches over high heat for 3–4 minutes, turning once until cooked through. Remove with a slotted spoon and drain on paper towels.

- While the fish is cooking, for the mayonnaise, mix together the sour cream and mayonnaise, then stir in the remaining ingredients and season with pepper. Place in a small serving bowl and serve with the hot goujons.

 Pan-Fried Cod with Lime and Caper Mayonnaise Toss 4 cod loin steaks, about 6 oz each, in 6 tablespoons all-purpose flour well seasoned with salt and pepper. Heat 4 tablespoons olive oil in a large, heavy skillet and cook over medium-high heat for 2–3 minutes on each side until golden and cooked through. Meanwhile, make the lime and caper mayonnaise as above. Serve the hot cod steaks with the creamy mayonnaise spooned over.

Lime and Chili Cod Loin Steaks with Potato Cubes Lightly toss 4 cod loin steaks, about 6 oz each, in 6 tablespoons all-purpose flour seasoned with salt and pepper. Dip into 2 beaten eggs in a shallow bowl and then 2 cups fresh white bread crumbs mixed with 1 teaspoon red pepper flakes. Place on a baking sheet. Cut 3 large baking potatoes into small cubes and toss in 2 tablespoons olive oil. Arrange between the fish on the baking sheet and place in a preheated oven, 400°F, for 20 minutes until browned and cooked through. Meanwhile, make the lime and caper mayonnaise as above. Serve alongside the fish and potato cubes.

30 Prosciutto and Pesto-Wrapped Angler Fish

Serves 4

4 pieces of angler fish tail, about 6 oz each
2 tablespoons green pesto
4 slices of prosciutto
2 tablespoons olive oil
1 lb fresh tagliatelle
1 bunch of scallions, trimmed and thinly sliced
1 cup cherry tomatoes, halved
4¼ cups baby spinach leaves
salt and pepper

- Spread the angler fish tails on one side with the pesto and tightly wrap each with 1 slice of prosciutto. Heat 1 tablespoon of the oil in a large, heavy skillet and cook the angler fish tails over medium heat, prosciutto-join down, for 3–4 minutes, then turn over and cook on the other side for 3–4 minutes until browned. Transfer to a roasting pan and place in a preheated oven, 400°F, for 10 minutes.

- Meanwhile, bring a large saucepan of lightly salted water to a boil and cook the tagliatelle for 3–4 minutes or until just tender, then drain. Heat the remaining oil in a large saucepan and cook the scallions over medium heat, stirring frequently, for 1–2 minutes until slightly softened. Add the cherry tomatoes and cook, stirring, for 2 minutes, then add the spinach and cook, tossing, for 1 minute until just wilted. Toss in the drained pasta and season generously with pepper.

- Serve the angler fish with the tagliatelle on warmed plates.

1 Boiled Salmon with Pesto and Bacon

Place 4 skinless salmon fillets, about 5 oz each, on a broiler pan and spread each with 1 teaspoon green pesto. Lay 4 bacon slices next to the salmon and broil the salmon and bacon for 6–8 minutes until the salmon is opaque and cooked through and the bacon is browned and crisp. Serve the salmon fillets on warmed serving plates with a bacon slice laid across each top.

2 Pesto Angler Fish and Vegetable

Skewers Cut 1¼ lb angler fish tail into 1 inch pieces. Divide the fish between 4 metal skewers, or bamboo skewers presoaked in cold water for 30 minutes, alternating with 12 cherry tomatoes, 2 zucchini, trimmed and cut into chunks, and 8 bay leaves. Mix 2 teaspoons each of green pesto and olive oil, and drizzle over the skewers. Cook under a preheated high broiler or over a barbecue for 15 minutes. Serve with a salad and some crusty bread.

2 Indian Seafood Biryani

Serves 4

4 eggs
1¼ cups basmati rice
1½ cups green beans, cut into
short lengths
2 tablespoons vegetable oil
2 onions, thinly sliced
3 tablespoons biryani curry paste
6 oz large cooked peeled shrimp
6 oz crab sticks, torn into shreds
6 tablespoons chopped fresh
cilantro
⅔ cup plain yogurt mixed with 1
teaspoon mint sauce
salt

- Bring a large saucepan of lightly salted water to a boil and cook the eggs and rice in the same pan for 10 minutes. Remove the eggs with a slotted spoon. Add the beans to the pan and cook with the rice for an additional 5 minutes until both are tender, then drain. While the beans and rice are cooking, rinse the eggs under cold running water, then shell and roughly chop.

- Meanwhile, heat the oil in a large, heavy skillet and cook the onions over medium heat, stirring occasionally, for 5 minutes. Add the curry paste and cook, stirring, for 1 minute. Add the shrimp and crab sticks and cook, stirring, for 2 minutes until hot.

- Add the drained rice and beans and cilantro and cook, stirring, for 1 minute more. Toss through the chopped eggs, then serve hot with the minted yogurt on the side.

10 Speedy Indian Shrimp Pilaff

Heat 1 tablespoon vegetable oil in a large skillet and cook 1 small grated onion, 2 grated zucchini and 6 tablespoons balti curry paste over medium heat, stirring frequently, for 3 minutes. Add 1⅓ cups frozen peas and cook, stirring frequently, for an additional 2 minutes. Add 14 oz cooked peeled shrimp and cook, stirring, for 2 minutes. Lastly, add 2½ cups store-bought ready-cooked pilau rice and heat through for 2 minutes. Serve sprinkled with 1 teaspoon finely chopped red chili and a handful of cilantro leaves.

30 Indian Salmon Biryani with Lentils

Mix 3 tablespoons biryani curry paste with 3 tablespoons plain yogurt. Pour over 4 skinless salmon steaks, about 5 oz each, cover, and refrigerate. Heat 1 tablespoon olive oil in a heavy saucepan and cook 1 chopped red onion over medium heat, stirring frequently, for 2 minutes. Add 2 crushed garlic cloves, 1 seeded, and finely chopped small red chili, 2 pinches of ground turmeric, 1 small cinnamon stick, 1 star anise, and the crushed seeds from 4 cardamom pods and cook, stirring, for 1 minute more. Add ½ cup rinsed green lentils and 2½ cups vegetable stock and simmer for 5 minutes. Add ¾ cup basmati rice and simmer for an additional 15 minutes. Ten minutes before the rice and lentils are cooked, heat ½ tablespoon olive oil in a skillet, shake off the marinade from the salmon, and cook over gentle heat for 2–3 minutes on each side, then flake into chunks. Remove the cinnamon stick and star anise from the rice and lentils. Mix in the flaked salmon and 3 tablespoons chopped fresh cilantro and serve immediately.

Tuna Pasta Gratin with Butternut Squash and Peas

Serves 4

8 oz dried penne
2 tablespoons olive oil
1 onion, chopped
1 butternut squash, about 12 oz, peeled, seeded, and roughly chopped into cubes
2 x 7 oz cans tuna in oil, drained and flaked
1¼ cups frozen peas, defrosted
2 tablespoons butter
3½ tablespoons all-purpose flour
1¼ cups milk
¾ cup sour cream
1 tablespoon Dijon mustard
½ cup cheddar cheese, grated
salt

- Bring a large saucepan of lightly salted water to a boil and cook the penne for 10–12 minutes until just tender, then drain.

- Meanwhile, heat the oil in a large skillet or wok and cook the onion and butternut squash over medium heat, stirring, for 8–10 minutes until softened and golden. Add the drained pasta to the pan and toss together with the tuna and peas.

- Melt the butter in a saucepan, add the flour, and cook over medium heat, stirring, for a few seconds. Remove from the heat and add the milk, a little at a time, stirring well between each addition. Return to the heat, then bring to a boil, stirring constantly, cooking until thickened. Beat in the sour cream and mustard. Remove from the heat and stir into the pasta mixture.

- Transfer the mixture to a large gratin dish and sprinkle with the grated cheddar. Cook under a preheated high broiler for 3–4 minutes until the sauce is bubbling and the cheese is browned. Serve with a simple salad.

10 **Three-Cheese and Tuna Pasta** Bring a large saucepan of salted water to a boil and cook 1 lb fresh tagliatelle for 3–4 minutes, then drain and add back to the pan. Meanwhile, heat through 1 garlic baguette according to the pack instructions. Add 1½ cups store-bought fresh three-cheese pasta sauce, 1 tablespoon Dijon mustard, 2 x 7 oz cans tuna in oil, drained and flaked, and 1¼ cups defrosted frozen peas to the pasta, and heat through until piping hot. Serve with the garlic bread.

20 **Tuna, Pasta, and Cannellini Bean Salad** Drain and reserve the oil from 2 x 7 oz cans tuna in oil. Drain and rinse a 13 oz can cannellini beans and add to 16 oz cooked chilled pasta shapes with the flaked tuna. Whisk together 3 tablespoons of the reserved tuna oil, 3 tablespoons olive oil, 2 crushed garlic cloves, 1 teaspoon English powdered mustard, the finely grated zest of 1 lemon, and pepper, then stir through the pasta mixture. Finish with a sprinkling of thinly sliced red onion and shavings of Parmesan cheese. Serve with warm ciabatta.

Creamy Scallops with Leeks

Serves 4

3½ tablespoons butter
16 shelled and cleaned scallops, halved
1 bacon slice, roughly snipped
3 leeks, trimmed, cleaned, and sliced
¾ cup sour cream
finely grated zest of 1 lemon
pepper
quick-cook long-grain rice, to serve

- Melt half the butter in a large, heavy-based frying pan and cook the scallops and bacon over high heat, stirring frequently, for 2 minutes until just golden and cooked through. Remove with a slotted spoon and keep warm.

- Add the remaining butter to the pan and cook the leeks over a medium heat, stirring occasionally, for 5 minutes until softened and lightly browned in places. Add the sour cream and lemon zest and season generously with pepper.

- Return the scallops to the pan and toss into the creamy leeks. Serve immediately with quick-cook rice.

---

20 Creamy Scallop, Leek, and Bacon Pasta Bring a large saucepan of lightly salted water to a boil and cook 7 oz dried fusilli for 10–12 minutes until just tender. Drain, return to the pan, and keep warm. Meanwhile, melt 2 tablespoons butter in a large, heavy skillet and cook 8 chopped bacon slices and 16 shelled and cleaned scallops, sliced in half, over medium heat, stirring gently, for 2 minutes. Add 4 trimmed, cleaned, and sliced leeks and cook, stirring frequently, for an additional 5 minutes. Keep warm. Heat 2 tablespoons butter in a saucepan, add 3½ tablespoons all-purpose flour and cook over medium heat, stirring, for a few seconds. Remove from the heat and add 1 cup milk, a little at a time, stirring well between each addition. Return to the heat, then bring to a boil, stirring constantly, cooking until thickened. Remove from the heat and stir in 4 tablespoons freshly grated Parmesan, then ¾ cup sour cream and 3 tablespoons chopped parsley. Add the scallop mixture and sauce to the drained pasta, toss well, and serve.

---

30 Scallop and Bacon Kebabs with Leeks Cut 10 bacon slices in half and wrap each around 20 shelled and cleaned small scallops. Thread onto 4 metal skewers. Mix 2 tablespoons olive oil with 1 tablespoon honey and brush over the bacon. Melt 2 tablespoons butter with 1 tablespoon olive oil in a skillet and cook 2 finely sliced leeks, stirring, for 6–8 minutes until soft and golden. Add 1 teaspoon each finely grated lemon zest and whole grain mustard and ¾ cup sour cream and heat for 2 minutes. Keep warm. Heat a griddle pan over high heat and cook the skewers for 2–3 minutes on each side until brown and cooked through. Serve on a bed of the creamy leeks.

30 Salmon, Leek and Pea Pie with Dill Mash

Serves 4

1 lb skinless salmon fillet
2 tablespoons butter
3½ tablespoons all-purpose flour
2¾ cups milk
3 large leeks, trimmed, cleaned, and sliced
¾ cup frozen peas, defrosted
2 x 1 lb containers ready-made fresh mashed potato
¾ cup roughly chopped dill weed
¼ cup freshly grated Parmesan cheese
salt and pepper

- Place the salmon in a microwave-proof container and pour over 2 tablespoons water. Cover and cook in a microwave oven on high for 3–4 minutes until the fish is opaque and cooked through. Set aside and then flake into large chunks.

- Melt the butter in a saucepan, add the flour, and cook over medium heat, stirring, for a few seconds. Remove from the heat and add the milk, a little at a time, stirring between each addition. Then bring to a boil, stirring, until thickened. Remove from the heat and season with salt and pepper.

- Add the leeks and peas to the sauce, then gently stir in the salmon. Transfer to a large gratin dish. Place the mashed potato in a large bowl and beat with 2 tablespoons water and two-thirds of the dill until soft and smooth. Spoon over the salmon mixture and sprinkle with the Parmesan. Place in a preheated oven, 400°F, for 10 minutes, then transfer to a preheated high broiler and cook for 5 minutes until the top is browned. Sprinkle with the remaining dill.

 10 Quick Salmon, Spinach, and Pea Mash Heat a 1½ cups fresh cheese sauce in a saucepan over medium heat for 5 minutes. Add ½ cup frozen chopped spinach and ½ cup frozen peas and heat, stirring, until the spinach has wilted. Stir in 2 x 7¼ oz cans red salmon, drained and flaked, and heat through briefly. Meanwhile, heat 2 x 1 lb containers ready-made fresh mashed potato following the package instructions until piping hot. Spoon the hot sauce over the mash and serve.

 20 Oven-Baked Salmon with Leeks and Cheese Place 4 skinless salmon fillets, about 5 oz each, in a roasting pan and season well. Melt 2 tablespoons butter in a large, heavy skillet and cook 1 trimmed, cleaned, and thinly sliced large leek over high heat, stirring frequently, for 3 minutes until softened. Spoon over the salmon fillets, then top each with 1 tablespoon freshly grated Parmesan cheese. Place in a preheated oven, 400°F, for 10–12 minutes until the fish is cooked through.

Sprinkle with chopped dill to serve.

Warm Bang Bang Shrimp Salad with Thai Noodles

Serves 4

4 oz Thai rice noodles

finely grated zest and juice of
1 lime

1 tablespoon sesame oil

1 cup snow peas

1 bird's eye chili, thinly sliced

1 inch piece of fresh ginger root,
peeled and roughly chopped

8 oz large cooked peeled shrimp

4 tablespoons smooth
peanut butter

4 tablespoons light soy sauce

⅔ cup boiling water

⅓ cup dried pineapple pieces,
roughly chopped

- Place the noodles in a heatproof bowl, cover with boiling water and allow to soak following the package instructions until tender. Drain well and toss with the lime zest.

- Meanwhile, heat the oil in a large wok or heavy skillet and stir-fry the snow peas, chili, and ginger over high heat for 2 minutes. Add the shrimp and stir-fry for 2 minutes or until hot. Place the peanut butter, lime juice, and soy sauce in a bowl, add the measurement water, and mix well. Pour into the pan and toss the ingredients together.

- Add the drained noodles and pineapple pieces and gently toss to coat all the ingredients in the sauce. Serve immediately in warmed serving bowls.

 Bang Bang Skewered Shrimp

Thread each of 8 small metal skewers with 3 large raw peeled shrimp. Cook under a preheated high broiler for 3 minutes on each side until they have turned pink. Meanwhile, in a bowl, mix 4 tablespoons each smooth peanut butter and light soy sauce with the juice of 1 lime. Serve the sauce in small, individual bowls alongside the skewered shrimp and 2 peeled carrots, 2 celery sticks, and ½ large cucumber, cut into matchsticks.

 Bang Bang Shrimp with Egg-Fried Rice

Bring a saucepan of lightly salted water to a boil and cook 1¼ cups easy-cook long-grain rice for 15 minutes until tender, then drain. Return to the pan, add ½ cup cooked peas, 2 trimmed and finely chopped scallions, ⅓ cup roasted peanuts, 1 beaten egg, and 2 tablespoons each sesame oil and light soy sauce, and cook over medium-high heat, stirring, until the egg is cooked. Set aside. Heat 1 tablespoon sesame oil in a large wok or heavy skillet and stir-fry 1 cup snow peas, 1 thinly sliced bird's eye chili and a 1 inch piece of fresh ginger root, peeled and roughly chopped, over medium-high heat for 2 minutes. Add 8 oz large cooked peeled shrimp and stir-fry for 2 minutes. In a bowl, mix 4 tablespoons each smooth peanut butter and light soy sauce with ⅔ cup boiling water, then blend in 1 tablespoon cornstarch. Add to the pan and heat, stirring, until thickened. Serve over the egg-fried rice.

30 Creamy Haddock Gratin

Serves 4

1¼ lb skinless haddock fillet
2½ cups milk
1 bay leaf
3 tablespoons butter
5 tablespoons all-purpose flour
2 oz Gruyère cheese, grated
½ teaspoon prepared English
  mustard
salad, to serve

For the topping

2 cups fresh white bread crumbs
1 oz Gruyère cheese, finely grated
finely grated zest of 1 lemon
2 tablespoons chopped parsley

- Place the haddock in a saucepan with the milk and bay leaf, bring to a boil and continue boiling for 3 minutes. Remove the fish with a slotted spoon, reserving the milk, and divide between 4 individual gratin dishes.

- In a separate saucepan, melt the butter, add the flour, and cook over medium heat, stirring, for a few seconds. Remove from the heat and add the reserved milk, a little at a time, stirring well between each addition. Return to the heat, then bring to a boil, stirring constantly, cooking until thickened. Remove from the heat and add the grated Gruyère and mustard.

- Pour the sauce over the fish, dividing it evenly between the dishes. Mix together the ingredients for the topping and sprinkle over the sauce. Place on the top shelf of a preheated oven, 425°F, for 10 minutes until the topping is golden and the sauce bubbling. Serve with a simple salad.

10 Haddock Ceviche

Chop 8 oz very fresh skinless haddock as finely as you can and place in a wide, shallow nonmetallic dish. Sprinkle with 1 teaspoon sea salt, ½ teaspoon dried oregano, and 5 tablespoons lime juice. Cover and allow to marinate for 8 minutes. Drain the fish, discarding the white milky liquid. Add 3 chopped scallions, 1 chopped green chili, and 4 tablespoons chopped fresh cilantro. Serve spoonfuls of the ceviche on pieces of toasted baguette.

20 Cheat's Crunchy Haddock Gratin

Place 1¼ lb skinless haddock fillet in a saucepan with 6 tablespoons milk and a bay leaf. Bring to a boil and continue boiling for 3 minutes. Meanwhile, gently heat through a 1½ cups store-bought fresh cheese sauce in a separate saucepan. Drain the fish well, discarding the milk, and transfer to a large gratin dish, then pour over the sauce. In a food processor, whiz together a package of cheese-flavored tortilla chips with 2 tablespoons chopped parsley until crumbs form. Sprinkle all over the sauce. Place on the top shelf of a preheated oven, 425°F, for 10 minutes until the topping is browned and the sauce bubbling.

Rich Tomato, Wine, and Fish Stew

Serves 4

2 x 13 oz jars tomato sauce with peppers and onion

⅔ cup white wine

1 tablespoon olive oil

12 oz skinless white fish fillets, torn or cut into chunks

6 oz raw peeled shrimp

½ cup parsley, chopped

pepper

- Place the tomato sauce, wine, and oil in a large, heavy saucepan and bring to a boil.

- Reduce the heat, add the fish and shrimp, and simmer for 7 minutes until the fish is opaque and cooked through and the shrimp have turned pink.

- Add the parsley and season with pepper, then serve in warmed serving bowls with warm crusty bread.

 Rich Salmon and Bacon Stew

Heat 1 tablespoon olive oil in a large, heavy saucepan and cook 6 roughly chopped bacon slices over high heat, stirring frequently, for about 3 minutes until browned. Add 2 x 13 oz jars tomato sauce with peppers and onion with ⅔ cup white wine and bring to a boil. Reduce the heat to a simmer and add 4 skinless salmon steaks, about 5 oz each, cut into chunky cubes, along with 1 cup cherry tomatoes and 3 tablespoons chopped rosemary leaves. Bring to a boil and then simmer briskly, uncovered, for 15 minutes until the salmon is cooked through and the cherry tomatoes are tender. Serve with warm crusty bread to mop up the juices.

 Mediterranean Fish Stew with Chunky Vegetables

Heat 1 tablespoon olive oil in a large, deep skillet and cook 2 trimmed and chunkily chopped zucchini, 1 cored and seeded, Romero red sweet pepper and 1 yellow bell pepper, each cut into chunks, and 1 finely chopped red onion over medium heat, stirring occasionally, for 8–10 minutes until softened. Add 1 lb mixed skinless white fish fillets, cut into chunks, 6 oz cooked peeled shrimp, 2 x 13 oz jars tomato pasta sauce and 1¼ cups white wine and cook, stirring very gently occasionally, for 10 minutes or until the fish is cooked through. Stir in ½ cup pitted black olives and serve in warmed serving bowls topped with 3 oz store-bought ready-made croutons.

Lemony Shrimp and Broccoli Stir-Fry

Serves 4

¾ cup easy-cook long-grain rice
8 oz tenderstem broccoli,
    trimmed and cut into 3 inch
    lengths
3 tablespoons vegetable oil
1 large red onion, sliced
1 bunch of scallions, trimmed and
    roughly chopped
8 oz cooked peeled shrimp
finely grated zest and juice of
    1 lemon
3 tablespoons light soy sauce
salt

- Bring a saucepan of lightly salted water to a boil and cook the rice for 10 minutes. Add the broccoli to the pan and cook with the rice for an additional 5 minutes until both are tender. Drain well and keep warm.

- Meanwhile, heat the oil in a large, heavy skillet or wok and cook the onion over medium-high heat, stirring frequently, for 5 minutes until softened. Add the scallions and shrimp and stir-fry for 4 minutes.

- Add the lemon zest and juice and soy sauce to the pan and stir well, then add the drained rice and broccoli and stir-fry for 1 minute until all the ingredients are piping hot and well mixed. Serve immediately.

 Shrimp and Broccoli Noodles
Bring a saucepan of water to a boil and cook 7 oz medium egg noodles for 3 minutes, then drain. Trim each stem of 8 oz tenderstem broccoli and cut lengthwise into 3. Heat 3 table-spoons vegetable oil in a large, heavy skillet or wok and stir-fry the broccoli with 1 roughly chopped bunch of scallions, 8 oz cooked peeled shrimp, and 2 small heads shredded bok choy over medium-high heat for 4 minutes. Add the finely grated zest and juice of 1 lemon and 3 tablespoons light soy sauce and stir well. Add the drained noodles and toss until piping hot.

 Duck, Shrimp and Broccoli Gingered Rice Bring a saucepan of lightly salted water to a boil and cook ¾ cup easy-cook long-grain rice for 10 minutes. Add the broccoli to the pan and cook with the rice for an additional 5 minutes until both are tender. Drain well and keep warm. Meanwhile, heat 2 tablespoons sunflower oil in a large, heavy skillet or wok, add 1 thinly sliced boneless duck breast, about 6 oz, and stir-fry over medium-high heat for 5 minutes. Remove with a slotted spoon. Add 1 large sliced red onion and cook, stirring frequently, for 5 minutes until softened. Add 1 bunch of trimmed and roughly chopped scallions and 8 oz cooked peeled shrimp and stir-fry for 4 minutes. Add a 1½ inch piece of fresh ginger root, peeled and grated, and 3 tablespoons light soy sauce and stir well. Return the duck to the pan with the rice and broccoli and stir-fry for 1 minute.

30 Jamaican Spiced Salmon with Corn and Okra

Serves 4

4 skinless salmon fillets, about
6 oz each
1 tablespoon Jamaican jerk
seasoning
4 ears corn, halved
3 tablespoons olive oil
1 red onion, sliced
8 oz okra, trimmed
3½ tablespoons butter
½ teaspoon paprika
½ teaspoon ground nutmeg
salt

- Rub each of the salmon fillets with the Jamaican jerk seasoning and set aside.

- Bring a large saucepan of lightly salted water to a boil and cook the corn pieces for 15 minutes until tender.

- Heat 2 tablespoons of the oil in a large, heavy saucepan and cook the onion over medium heat, stirring frequently, for 2 minutes. Add the okra and cook, stirring frequently, for 4 minutes until beginning to soften. Drain the corn well, add to the pan with the butter and spices, and toss for an additional 2–3 minutes until lightly browned in places.

- Meanwhile, heat the remaining tablespoon of oil in a large, heavy skillet and cook the salmon fillets, spice-side down, over medium heat for 3–4 minutes, then turn over and cook for an additional 2 minutes until cooked through. Serve hot with the corn and okra mixture.

 Warm Jamaican Spiced Salmon Salad

Rub 4 skinless salmon fillets, about 6 oz each, with 1 tablespoon Jamaican jerk seasoning. Heat 1 tablespoon olive oil in a large, heavy skillet and cook the salmon fillets, spice-side down, over medium heat for 3–4 minutes, then turn over and cook for an additional 2 minutes until cooked through. Divide 2½ cups mixed salad leaves between 4 serving plates. Drain a 7 oz can corn kernels and thinly slice ½ red onion. Divide between the plates. Flake the salmon over the salad and serve with lime wedges for squeezing over.

2 **Short-Cut Jamaican Spiced Salmon**

Follow the recipe above, but instead of boiling the corn pieces for 15 minutes, place in a microwave-proof bowl with 4 tablespoons water and cover. Cook in a microwave oven on high for 6 minutes.

Shrimp Spaghetti with Tomato, Garlic, and Basil Sauce

Serves 4

1 lb fresh spaghetti
2 tablespoons olive oil
2 garlic cloves, sliced
2 x 13 oz cans chopped tomatoes
3 tablespoons sundried tomato paste
8 oz large cooked peeled shrimp
⅔ cup basil, roughly chopped
salt and pepper
freshly grated Parmesan cheese, to serve (optional)

- Bring a large saucepan of lightly salted water to a boil and cook the spaghetti for 3 minutes or until just tender, then drain.

- Meanwhile, heat the oil in a large, heavy skillet and cook the garlic over medium heat for a few seconds to flavor the oil, then add the tomatoes and tomato paste and cook, stirring occasionally, for 5 minutes until thickened.

- Add the shrimp and basil, stir through, and heat through for 1–2 minutes until the shrimp are piping hot. Season generously with pepper, then add the drained pasta and toss with the sauce to mix.

- Serve in warmed serving bowls, sprinkled with freshly grated Parmesan cheese, if desired.

---

2 **Spicy Tomato, Garlic, Seafood, and Bacon Pasta** Bring a large saucepan of lightly salted water to a boil and cook 1 lb fresh spaghetti for 3 minutes or until just tender. Drain and return to the pan. Heat 2 tablespoons olive oil in a large, heavy skillet and cook 1 finely chopped red chili and 2 sliced garlic cloves over medium heat, stirring, for 2 minutes. Add 8 roughly chopped bacon slices and cook, stirring frequently, for an additional 2 minutes. Add 7 oz well-drained prepared small scallops and 7 oz large cooked peeled shrimp and cook over high heat, stirring frequently, for 3–4 minutes.

Add 2 x 13 oz cans chopped tomatoes and 3 tablespoons sundried tomato paste and cook, stirring occasionally, for 5 minutes until thickened. Stir in ¾ cup chopped parsley, then add to the drained pasta and toss to coat.

3 **Shrimp, Tomato and Garlic Bake** Cook 1 lb fresh penne per package instructions, then drain. Meanwhile, heat 2 tablespoons olive oil in a large pan and cook 2 sliced garlic cloves over medium heat, stirring, for 2 minutes. Add 6 tablespoons sundried tomato paste and 2 x 13 oz cans chopped tomatoes. Bring to a boil, then simmer, uncovered, for 10 minutes until the sauce has reduced by a quarter. Add 4 tablespoons chopped basil, then toss the pasta into the sauce. Transfer to a gratin dish and sprinkle with 1 cup grated Gruyère cheese. Cook under a high broiler for 5 minutes until golden.

10 Pan-Fried Cod and Fries with Lemon Mayo and Dill

Serves 4

4 tablespoons vegetable oil

4 baking potatoes, peeled and cut into cubes

1 tablespoon olive oil

4 pieces of cod loin, about 5 oz each

juice and finely grated zest of 1 lemon

4 tablespoons snipped dill weed

6 tablespoons mayonnaise

salt and pepper

- Heat the oil in a large, heavy skillet and cook the potatoes over medium-high heat, turning frequently, for 7–10 minutes until golden and crisp.

- Meanwhile, heat the olive oil in a separate large skillet and cook the cod loins over high heat for 3–5 minutes, turning once, until golden and cooked through. Squeeze the lemon juice over the fish and season with salt and pepper.

- Mix the lemon zest and half the dill into the mayonnaise and serve with the fish and fries. Sprinkle the remaining dill over the fish to serve.

 2 Pan-Fried Cod and Prosciutto with Sweet Potatoes Heat 3 tablespoons vegetable oil in a large, heavy skillet and cook 4 peeled and cubed sweet potatoes over medium-high heat, turning frequently, for 8–10 minutes until browned and soft. Keep warm. Meanwhile, wrap each of 4 pieces of cod loin, about 5 oz each, with a slice of prosciutto. Heat 1 tablespoon vegetable oil in a separate skillet and cook the fish over medium-high heat, turning occasionally, for 8–10 minutes until golden and cooked through. Mix 6 tablespoons mayonnaise with the finely grated zest of ½ lemon and 3 tablespoons chopped parsley. Serve with the potatoes and pan-fried cod.

 3 Roasted Cod Wrapped in Bacon with Oven Fries Cut 4 peeled baking potatoes into fry-sized pieces and toss with 2 tablespoons vegetable oil. Spread over a baking sheet in a single layer, then place in a preheated oven, 425°F, for 20 minutes until golden and soft. Meanwhile, wrap each of 4 pieces of cod loin, about 5 oz each, with a Canadian bacon slice, adding 2–3 basil leaves between the fish and the bacon. Place in a roasting pan and season generously. Place in the oven with the potatoes for 15 minutes until the fish is opaque and cooked through. Serve with the fries, sprinkled with chopped parsley, if desired.

30 Garlic and Tomato Seafood Spaghetti

Serves 4

8 oz dried spaghetti
3 tablespoons olive oil
2 garlic cloves, sliced
3 shallots, cut into slim wedges
1 celery stick, thinly sliced
4 tomatoes, roughly chopped
13 oz can chopped tomatoes
⅔ cup white wine
1 tablespoon chopped thyme
3 tablespoons chopped parsley
8 oz large cooked peeled shrimp
8 oz package frozen raw mixed
  seafood, defrosted
salt
warm crusty bread, to serve
  (optional)

- Bring a large saucepan of lightly salted water to a boil and cook the spaghetti for 8–10 minutes until just tender. Drain and keep warm.

- Meanwhile, heat the oil in a large, heavy skillet and cook the garlic, shallots, and celery over medium heat, stirring occasionally, for 3–4 minutes until slightly softened. Add the fresh tomatoes, increase the heat, and cook, stirring occasionally, for 2–3 minutes. Stir in the canned tomatoes and wine.

- Bring the tomato mixture to a boil, then reduce the heat slightly to a brisk simmer and cook for 8–10 minutes until the sauce has reduced by one-third. Add the herbs, shrimp and mixed seafood and cook for 3–4 minutes until the seafood is opaque and all is piping hot. Add the drained spaghetti and toss well to coat in the sauce.

- Serve in warmed serving bowls with warm crusty bread to mop up the juices, if desired.

10 Speedy Seafood Pot

Heat 2 tablespoons butter with a drop of wok oil in a wok with a lid and stir-fry 8 oz large cooked peeled shrimp and a 8 oz package frozen cooked mixed seafood over high heat until the seafood is opaque. Stir in ½ cup white wine, cover, shake the pan, and allow to cook for 3 minutes. Add 4 tablespoons sherry, re-cover, and cook for an additional 3 minutes, shaking the pan occasionally. Serve in the pan, sprinkled with chopped parsley, with warm crusty bread.

20 Seafood Paella

Melt 2 tablespoons butter in a large, nonstick skillet and cook 1 finely chopped onion, a pinch of saffron threads, 2 cored, seeded, and diced red bell peppers and 2 chopped tomatoes over medium heat, stirring occasionally, for 3–4 minutes until softened. Add 1¼ cups quick-cook long-grain rice, 8 oz large raw peeled shrimp, a 8 oz package defrosted frozen raw mixed seafood, and 2 tablespoons white wine and simmer for 3 minutes. Add ⅔ cup vegetable stock and simmer for an additional 5–6 minutes until the shrimp have turned pink, the seafood is opaque, and the rice is tender. Stir in 3 tablespoons chopped parsley. Serve immediately, garnished with parsley sprigs and lemon wedges.

30 Cheesy Tuna and Corn Fishcakes

Serves 4

10 oz ready-made fresh mashed potato

½ teaspoon ground black pepper

½ cup finely grated cheddar cheese,

7 oz can tuna in oil, drained and flaked

½ cup frozen corn kernels, defrosted

3 tablespoons chopped parsley

3 cups fresh whole-wheat bread crumbs

1 egg

vegetable oil, for pan-frying

To serve

store-bought hollandaise sauce

arugula salad dressed with lemon juice

- Place the mashed potato in a bowl with the pepper and cheddar and beat well until smooth. Stir in the tuna, corn, and parsley and mix well. Shape into 8 patties.

- Place the bread crumbs on a plate. Beat the egg in a shallow bowl. Dip each of the patties in the egg and lightly brush, then lightly coat in the breadcrumbs.

- Heat 6–8 tablespoons vegetable oil in a large, heavy skillet and cook the fishcakes in 2 batches over medium-high heat for 4–5 minutes, turning once, until golden and crisp. Remove with a spatula, drain on kitchen paper towels, and keep the first batch warm while cooking the remainder.

- Serve the fishcakes hot with spoonfuls of hollandaise sauce and a simple arugula salad dressed with lemon juice.

10 Tuna and Corn Melts

Mix together a 7 oz can tuna in oil, drained and flaked, ½ cup defrosted frozen corn kernels, and 2 tablespoons mayonnaise. Cut a ciabatta loaf in half lengthwise and then each piece in half again. Spread each piece of bread with the tuna mixture and sprinkle ¼ cup cheddar cheese over the top. Cook under a preheated medium-high broiler for 2 minutes or until golden. Serve immediately with a green salad.

20 Creamy Tuna and Corn Fusilli

Bring a large saucepan of lightly salted water to a boil and cook 8 oz dried fusilli for 10–12 minutes until just tender, then drain. Meanwhile, melt 2 tablespoons butter in a saucepan, add 3½ tablespoons all-purpose flour, and cook over medium heat, stirring, for a few seconds. Remove from the heat and add 1¼ cups milk, a little at a time, stirring well between each addition. Add ½ cup grated cheddar cheese. Return to the heat, then bring to a boil, stirring constantly, cooking until thickened. Add a 7 oz can tuna in oil, drained and flaked, ½ cup defrosted frozen corn kernels, and 3 tablespoons chopped parsley to the sauce. Drain the pasta, toss with the sauce, and serve immediately in warmed bowls.

Cajun Spiced Salmon Frittata with Peppers

Serves 4

1 tablespoon olive oil

1 red bell pepper, cored, seeded, and cut into chunks

1 green bell pepper, cored, seeded, and cut into chunks

1 small onion, sliced

1 small red chili, finely chopped

6 tablespoons chopped fresh cilantro, plus extra to garnish

8 oz skinless salmon fillets

1 inch piece of fresh ginger root, peeled and roughly chopped

2 teaspoons Cajun spice mix

6 eggs

pepper

salad, to serve

- Heat the oil in a 9 inch nonstick skillet and cook the peppers, onion, and chili over medium heat, stirring occasionally, for 3–4 minutes until beginning to soften. Stir in the cilantro, then make a well in the center of the pan, add the salmon fillets, and cook for 3–4 minutes, turning once, until almost cooked through.

- Flake the fillets into chunky pieces in the pan, then add the ginger and spice mix to the pan and gently toss all the ingredients together. Beat the eggs in a bowl and season with a little pepper. Pour over the vegetables and salmon and gently cook for 3–4 minutes until the base of the frittata is set.

- Place the pan under a preheated medium broiler, making sure that the pan handle is turned away from the heat, and cook for 4–5 minutes until the top is golden and set. Cut into wedges and serve with a simple salad.

 Simple Cajun Salmon Mix a squeeze of ginger paste with 2 teaspoons Cajun spice mix and rub into the flesh of 8 oz skinless salmon fillets. Heat 3 tablespoons olive oil in a large skillet and cook the salmon over medium heat for 9 minutes, turning halfway through cooking until the fish is cooked through. Serve with bread and salad.

 Cajun Salmon Fishcakes Heat 1 tablespoon olive oil in a large, heavy skillet and cook 1 cored, seeded, and diced red bell pepper, 1 small diced onion, and 8 oz skinless salmon fillets for 9 minutes, turning halfway through cooking until cooked through. Flake the salmon into small pieces in the pan, then place in a large bowl with the pepper and onion and 8 oz instant mashed potato, made up according to the package instructions. Mix together with 2 teaspoons Cajun spice mix, a 1 inch piece of fresh ginger root, peeled and grated, 6 tablespoons chopped fresh cilantro, and 1 beaten egg. Shape into 8 large fishcakes. Heat 3 tablespoons olive oil in the skillet and cook over medium-high heat for about 5 minutes on each side until browned. Serve with oven fries and salad.

Shrimp and Parmesan Tagliatelle with Wilted Spinach

Serves 4

8 oz dried tagliatelle
2 tablespoons olive oil
1 red onion, thinly sliced
1 bunch of scallions, trimmed and
  sliced
1 garlic clove, sliced
10 oz raw peeled shrimp
4¼ cups baby spinach leaves
1¾ cups tubs mascarpone cheese
½ cup freshly grated
  Parmesan cheese
salt and pepper
warm crusty whole-wheat bread,
  to serve (optional)

- Bring a large saucepan of lightly salted water to a boil and cook the tagliatelle for 8–10 minutes until just tender, then drain.

- Meanwhile, heat the oil in a large, heavy skillet and cook the onion over medium heat, stirring occasionally, for 5 minutes until softened. Add the scallions and garlic and cook, stirring frequently, for 2 minutes. Add the shrimp and cook over high heat, stirring, for 2 minutes, then add the spinach leaves and cook, stirring constantly, for 1–2 minutes until the spinach has wilted and the shrimp have turned pink.

- Add the mascarpone and stir through until melted and hot. Season with plenty of pepper, then add the Parmesan and drained pasta. Heat through, tossing, for 1–2 minutes until piping hot.

- Serve in warmed serving bowls with warm crusty whole-wheat bread, if desired.

 Shrimp Noodle Stir-Fry

Cook 7 oz egg noodles according to package instructions, then drain. Meanwhile, heat 2 tablespoons peanut oil in a large wok and stir-fry 1 chopped red chili and 2 sliced garlic cloves over high heat for 1 minute. Add 1 lb cooked peeled shrimp and stir-fry for 3 minutes until hot. Add 10 oz ready-prepared mixed stir-fry vegetables and 2 tablespoons each light soy sauce and sweet chili sauce. Add the drained noodles and toss until piping hot.

 Shrimp with Chili, Spinach, and Cheese Place 1 lb raw peeled shrimp in a nonmetallic bowl and add the juice of 2 limes and a splash of Tabasco sauce. Cover and allow to marinate for 10 minutes. Meanwhile, heat 2 tablespoons olive oil in a large, heavy skillet and cook 2 thinly sliced red onions and 2 crushed garlic cloves over medium heat, stirring frequently, for about 3 minutes. Add 1 teaspoon dried red pepper flakes and cook, stirring, for an additional 2 minutes. Transfer to a large gratin dish and sprinkle with a well-drained 13 oz can cooked spinach. Drain the shrimp and add to the dish. Season well, then pour over ¾ cup heavy cream and sprinkle 1 cup each ready-grated mozzarella cheese and freshly grated Parmesan cheese on top. Cook under a preheated high broiler for about 10 minutes until browned. Serve sprinkled with fresh cilantro leaves and a loaf of fresh French bread.

30 Roasted Smoked Haddock with Mash and Poached Eggs

Serves 4

1½ lb potatoes, peeled and roughly chopped

5 tablespoons milk

3½ tablespoons butter

4 tablespoons chopped flat-leaf parsley

4 pieces of smoked haddock, about 8 oz each

4–5 drops lemon juice or malt vinegar

4 eggs

¾ cup ready-made hollandaise sauce

salt and pepper

- Bring a large saucepan of lightly salted water to a boil and cook the potatoes for 20 minutes until tender. Drain, return to the pan, and mash with the milk and butter. Season generously with pepper and stir through the parsley.

- Meanwhile, place the fish in a roasting pan and place in a preheated oven, 400°F, for 15 minutes until opaque and cooked through.

- Half-fill a saucepan with water and bring to a boil. Once at a rolling boil, add the lemon juice or vinegar. Stir the water, then break an egg into the water as it's moving and cook the egg for 1–2 minutes until the white is set and the yolk cooked to your liking. Remove with a slotted spoon and keep warm while cooking the remaining eggs in the same way.

- Divide the mash between 4 warmed serving plates, top each serving with a fish fillet and then place a poached egg on the top. Spoon over the hollandaise, or serve in a separate dish, and finish with a gzesting of black pepper.

---

10 Smoked Salmon and Egg Muffins

Cook 4 poached eggs as above. Meanwhile, split and lightly toast 4 English muffins. Place on serving plates and divide 8 oz smoked salmon slices between the toasted muffins. Top each serving with a poached egg, spoon over ¾ cup ready-made hollandaise sauce and sprinkle with chopped parsley.

20 Smoked Haddock Kedgeree with Eggs

Cook ¾ cup easy-cook basmati rice in a saucepan of lightly salted boiling water for 15 minutes until tender, then drain. Meanwhile, boil 4 eggs in a saucepan of water for 6 minutes, then drain and cool under cold running water. Place 8 oz smoked haddock in a microwave-proof dish, cover, and cook in a microwave oven on high for 2–3 minutes. Skin and flake the haddock, discarding any bones.

Melt 1 tablespoon butter in a saucepan and cook ½ finely chopped onion over gentle heat, stirring frequently, for about 3 minutes until softened. Add 2 teaspoons mild curry paste and cook, stirring, for 1–2 minutes. Add the cooked rice and fish, and season well. Stir over medium heat for about 2 minutes until hot, then stir in 4 tablespoons chopped flat-leaf parsley and the juice of ½ lemon. Peel the eggs, quarter, and arrange on top of the kedgeree to serve.

 # Cherry Tomato and Cod Stir-Fry with Bacon

Serves 4

2 tablespoons olive oil
1 bunch of scallions, trimmed and
   roughly chopped
1 garlic clove, thinly sliced
6 oz bacon, chopped
1 cup cherry tomatoes, halved
12 oz skinless cod, coley,
   or haddock fillet, cut into cubes
finely grated zest of 1 lemon
2 large handfuls of spinach leaves
5 oz feta cheese, crumbled
warm crusty bread, to serve

- Heat the oil in a large, heavy skillet and cook the scallions, garlic, and bacon over high heat, stirring frequently, for 2–3 minutes until the onions are softened and the bacon is browned. Add the tomatoes and fish, reduce the heat, and cook, stirring gently and tossing occasionally so that the fish cubes stay intact as much as possible, for 3–4 minutes until the fish is opaque and cooked through.

- Sprinkle with the lemon zest and spinach leaves, cover, and cook for 1–2 minutes until the spinach has wilted, then gently fold the ingredients together. Sprinkle with the feta.

- Serve piled onto warmed serving plates with warm crusty bread to mop up the juices.

 ### Cod, Tomato, and Bacon Gratin

Melt 1 tablespoon butter with 1 tablespoon olive oil in a skillet and cook 1 bunch of trimmed and chopped scallions and 6 chopped Canadian bacon slices over high heat, stirring frequently, for 2 minutes. Add 12 oz cubed skinless cod fillet and cook, stirring gently, for 2 minutes. Transfer to a heat-proof serving dish and sprinkle with 4 tablespoons bread crumbs mixed with 2 tablespoons grated cheddar cheese and 1 tablespoon chopped parsley. Top with a handful of halved cherry tomatoes. Cook under a high broiler for 2 minutes. Serve with crusty French bread.

 ### Tomato and Smoked Cod Bake

Heat 1 tablespoon olive oil in a heavy-based skillet and cook 4 trimmed, cleaned, and sliced leeks, 1 sliced garlic clove, and 6 oz chopped bacon over high heat, stirring frequently, for 3 minutes. Transfer to an ovenproof dish with 12 oz cubed skinless smoked cod and 4 sliced beef tomatoes. Season with pepper and toss to mix. Toast 4 slices of white bread, then whiz in a processor to make breadcrumbs. In a small bowl, mix the bread crumbs with 3 tablespoons grated cheddar cheese and 1 tablespoon chopped parsley. Sprinkle over the fish and place in a preheated oven, 350°F, for 25 minutes. Serve with warm crusty bread.

 # Sticky Honey and Chili Salmon Skewers with Rice

Serves 4

4 tablespoons sweet chili sauce
4 tablespoons honey
4 tablespoons chopped cilantro
2 scallions, finely sliced
1 tablespoon sesame oil
1 lb skinless salmon fillet, cut
  into chunks
salt and pepper

For the rice

1¼ cups easy-cook basmati rice
2 tablespoons sesame oil
1 red onion, thinly sliced
6 scallions, roughly chopped
1¾ cups sugar snap peas,
  shredded
4 tablespoons chopped cilantro

- Bring a saucepan of salted water to a boil and cook the rice for 15 minutes until just tender, then drain. Keep warm.

- Meanwhile, mix together the chili sauce, honey, cilantro, scallions and oil in a large bowl. Add the salmon chunks and toss well to coat. Season with a little pepper.

- Thread the salmon onto 8 metal skewers. Place on a broiler rack lined with foil and cook under a preheated medium broiler for 7–8 minutes, turning 2–3 times, until lightly charred in places and cooked through.

- Meanwhile, heat the oil in a large wok or heavy skillet and stir-fry the red onion over high heat for 3 minutes. Add the scallions and sugar snap peas and stir-fry for an additional 2 minutes until just beginning to soften. Add the drained rice and stir-fry for 2 minutes, then add the cilantro and toss well. Spoon the rice onto serving plates and arrange the hot salmon skewers on top.

 ### Honey and Mustard Salmon with Zucchini Ribbons

In a bowl, mix together 1 tablespoon each whole grain mustard and light soy sauce, the juice of 1 lemon, and 1 teaspoon honey. Place 4 salmon fillets on a foil-lined broiler rack and brush over the honey mixture. Cook the salmon under a preheated medium-high broiler for 8 minutes or until browned and cooked through. Remove and serve with steamed zucchini ribbons and lemon wedges for squeezing over.

 ### Honey-Seared Salmon with Cilantro Noodles

Cook 7 oz medium egg noodles in a saucepan of boiling water for about 4 minutes until tender. Drain and rinse under cold running water until cool, then drain again. Combine the noodles with 4 tablespoons each chopped fresh cilantro, mint, and basil and 2 trimmed and shredded zucchini. Add 2 tablespoons light soy sauce and 1 tablespoon lime juice and toss with the noodles to coat. Cut 1 lb skinless salmon fillet into ¾ inch wide strips and toss with 2 tablespoons honey and pepper. Heat a large, nonstick skillet over high heat and cook the salmon for 2 minutes on each side or until the honey coating is browned. To serve, place the noodles on serving plates and top with the salmon strips.

30 Black Olive and Sunblush Tomato Risotto with Cod

Serves 4

4 pieces of cod loin, about 6 oz each

2 tablespoons olive oil

1 red onion, finely chopped

½ cup pitted black olives, roughly chopped

½ cup sunblush tomatoes, roughly chopped

1¼ cups Arborio risotto rice

3¾ cups hot rich chicken stock

½ cup freshly grated Parmesan cheese

1 cup basil, roughly chopped

pepper

- Place the cod pieces in a roasting pan and drizzle with 1 tablespoon of the oil. Season with pepper. Set aside.

- Heat the remaining tablespoon of oil in a large, heavy skillet and cook the onion over medium heat, stirring frequently, for 3–4 minutes until softened. Add the olives and tomatoes and cook, stirring, for 1 minute. Add the rice, then pour in half the stock. Bring to a boil, then reduce the heat and simmer gently, stirring occasionally, for 5–6 minutes until almost all the stock has been absorbed.

- Place the cod in a preheated oven, 400°F, for 15 minutes until cooked through. Meanwhile, stir the remaining stock into the rice and continue simmering, stirring occasionally, until almost all the stock has been absorbed and the rice is tender. Remove from the heat and stir in the Parmesan and basil. Season with pepper.

- Serve the risotto on warmed serving plates with the roasted cod on top.

---

10 Parmesan Cod Fillets with Avocado and Cress Salad

Place 4 tablespoons all-purpose flour in a shallow dish and season with salt and pepper. Dust 4 cod fillets, about 5 oz each, with the seasoned flour, then dip the fish into 2 eggs beaten in a shallow bowl and finally dust with ¾ cup finely grated Parmesan cheese, making sure that the fish is well covered. Heat 1 tablespoon olive oil in a large, heavy skillet and cook the cod fillets over high heat for 2 minutes on each side, depending on their thickness, until browned and cooked through. Meanwhile, toss together 2 pitted, peeled, and sliced ripe avocados and 1 container cress with 2 tablespoons extra virgin olive oil and the juice of 1 lemon. Serve with the cod fillets.

20 Cod with Sunblush Tomatoes, Basil, and Mozzarella

Place 4 pieces of cod loin, about 6 oz each, in an oiled roasting pan. Drizzle with olive oil and season with salt and pepper. Top with ½ cup roughly chopped sunblush tomatoes, 1 cup basil, chopped, and 2 finely sliced balls of mozzarella, about 5 oz. Sprinkle over ½ cup grated Parmesan cheese, drizzle with more olive oil, and place on the top shelf of a preheated oven, 425°F, for 15 minutes until golden.

QuickCook

Fast and Veggie

Recipes listed by cooking time

30

20

Thai Vegetable Curry

Serves 4

1 lb butternut squash, peeled, seeded, and cut into chunks

2 red bell peppers, cored, seeded, and cut into chunks

6 oz baby corn, halved

⅔ cup cauliflower florets

2 tablespoons Thai green curry paste

3¼ cups coconut milk

⅔ cup vegetable stock

1¾ cups sugar snap peas

2 tablespoons cold water

1 tablespoon cornstarch

4 tablespoons chopped fresh cilantro

cooked Thai jasmine rice, to serve

- Place the squash, red peppers, corn, and cauliflower in a large, heavy saucepan, add the curry paste, coconut milk, and stock, and bring to a boil. Reduce the heat, cover with a lid, and simmer for 15 minutes until the vegetables are tender, adding the sugar snap peas for the final 5 minutes of cooking.

- Blend the measurement water with the cornstarch, add to the curry, and cook, stirring constantly, until it thickens slightly. Stir in the cilantro and serve with Thai jasmine rice, if desired.

 Thai Corn and Cauliflower Curried Soup Dice ⅔ cup cauliflower florets and place in a large, heavy saucepan with 3¼ cups canned coconut milk, 2 tablespoons Thai green curry paste, ⅔ cup vegetable stock, and 6 oz halved baby corn. Cook, stirring occasionally, for 9 minutes over high heat. Stir in 4 tablespoons chopped fresh cilantro before serving.

 Malaysian Vegetable Curry In a food processor, combine 3 garlic cloves, 2 red chilies, 2 lemon grass stalks, a 1½ inch piece of fresh ginger root, peeled, 3 chopped shallots, 3 tablespoons peanut oil, 1 tablespoon palm sugar, and 1 teaspoon each ground turmeric and ground cinnamon to make a curry paste. Place 1 lb butternut squash, peeled, seeded, and cut into chunks, 2 red bell peppers, cut into chunks, 6 oz halved baby corn, and ⅔ cup cauliflower florets in a large, heavy saucepan, add the curry paste, 2 star anise, 2 dried kaffir lime leaves, 3¼ cups canned coconut milk, and ⅔ cup vegetable stock and bring to a boil. Reduce the heat, cover, and simmer for 15 minutes until the vegetables are tender, adding 3¾ cups sugar snap peas for the final 5 minutes. Blend 2 tablespoons cold water with 1 tablespoon cornstarch, add to the curry, and cook, stirring constantly, until it thickens slightly. Stir in 4 tablespoons chopped fresh cilantro and serve with cooked Thai jasmine rice, if desired.

3 Spicy Bean Burgers with Tomato Salsa

Serves 4

13 oz can red kidney beans
4 tablespoons chopped cilantro
1 small red chili, finely chopped
1 tablespoon ground paprika
½ teaspoon ground cumin
½ teaspoon ground cilantro
3 scallions, chopped
1 egg yolk
2 cups white bread crumbs
vegetable oil, for pan-frying

For the salsa

2 tomatoes, finely chopped
1 tablespoon olive oil
2 tablespoons chopped cilantro
2 scallions, roughly chopped
pepper

To serve

4 soft whole-wheat buns
arugula leaves

- Drain the kidney beans and place in a bowl and mash with a fork until soft but still retaining some bean shapes. Add the cilantro, half the chili, the ground spices, scallions, egg yolk, and bread crumbs and mix well. Form into 4 patties.

- Heat 3–4 tablespoons vegetable oil in a large, heavy skillet and cook the burgers over medium-high heat for 2–3 minutes on each side until browned. Keep warm while making the salsa.

- For the salsa, place the tomatoes, olive oil, and cilantro in a bowl, add the remaining chili and the scallions and stir well to mix. Season with a little pepper.

- Serve each burger in a soft whole-wheat bun with a few arugula leaves and some of the tomato salsa.

 Quick Bean and Pasta Soup

Place a drained 13 oz can mixed beans in a saucepan along with 1¼ cups store-bought tomato-based pasta sauce and 3 cups hot vegetable stock. Bring to a boil, then stir in 4 oz dried mini pasta shapes of your choice and cook according to the package instructions until just tender. Serve with some warm crusty bread rolls.

 Tortilla Bean Cheesecake

Heat 1 teaspoon olive oil in a large saucepan and cook 1 chopped onion over medium heat, stirring frequently, for 3 minutes. Stir in ½ teaspoon chili powder and a 13 oz can chopped tomatoes with herbs, then cook over high heat for 5 minutes until slightly thickened. Add 7 oz frozen mixed vegetables and cook for an additional 3 minutes. Stir through a drained 13 oz can red kidney beans. Take 5 soft flour tortillas and place one on a heatproof plate, spread with a little of the sauce, and sprinkle with a handful of grated cheddar cheese. Continue layering the tortillas, sauce, and cheese, finishing with a sprinkling of cheese. Set the plate on a baking sheet and place in a preheated oven, 350°F, for 10 minutes until the cheese has melted. Cut into wedges and serve with sour cream and chopped scallions.

30 Roasted Vegetable Pasta with Garlic and Herb Sauce

Serves 4

2 zucchini, trimmed and cut into chunks

1 eggplant, trimmed and cut into chunks

1 large red onion, cut into chunks

4 tablespoons olive oil

1 large onion, chopped

2 garlic cloves, sliced

1 lb tomatoes, roughly chopped

3 tablespoons tomato paste

4 tablespoons chopped parsley

1 tablespoon chopped rosemary leaves

⅔ cup water

8 oz dried fusilli

salt

warm crusty bread, to serve (optional)

- Place the zucchini, eggplant, and onion in a large roasting pan and toss with 3 tablespoons of the olive oil. Place in a preheated oven, 425°F, for 20 minutes until tender and lightly charred in places.

- Meanwhile, heat the remaining tablespoon of oil in a large, heavy skillet and cook the onion and garlic over medium-high heat, stirring frequently, for 3 minutes until softened. Add the tomatoes and cook, stirring occasionally, for an additional 10 minutes. Add the tomato paste, herbs, and measurement water and bring to a boil, then reduce the heat and simmer for 5 minutes.

- While the sauce is cooking, bring a large saucepan of lightly salted water to a boil and cook the fusilli for 10–12 minutes until just tender, then drain.

- Add the roasted vegetables to the tomato sauce along with the drained pasta and toss well together. Serve in warmed serving bowls, with warm crusty bread, if desired.

---

10 Creamy Roasted Vegetable Pasta

Cook 1 lb fresh fusilli in a large saucepan of lightly salted boiling water for 3–4 minutes or until just tender. Drain, return to the pan, and stir in 1¼ cups store-bought roasted vegetable pasta sauce, a 10 oz jar artichoke antipasti, drained well, and 1 tablespoon chopped rosemary leaves. Heat through over medium heat. Serve immediately, sprinkled with freshly grated Parmesan cheese, with garlic bread.

20 Roasted Vegetable Couscous with Feta

Place 2 zucchini and 1 eggplant, each trimmed and cut into chunks, and 1 large red onion, cut into chunks, in a large roasting pan and toss with 3 tablespoons olive oil. Place in a preheated oven, 425°F, for 20 minutes until tender and lightly charred in places. Meanwhile, place 1 cup couscous in a bowl and add enough warm water to cover by ½ inch. Mix in ½ teaspoon salt and allow the couscous to absorb the water for 15 minutes. Fluff up the couscous with a fork and mix in 1 tablespoon olive oil and the juice of ½ lemon. Stir in the roasted vegetables and season with salt and pepper, then crumble over 7 oz feta cheese and sprinkle with some shredded basil.

Egg, Basil, and Cheese Salad with Cherry Tomatoes

Serves 4

2 tablespoons olive oil

2 eggs, beaten

½ cup basil, roughly chopped

7 oz feta cheese, drained and crumbled

1 cup cherry plum tomatoes, halved

2 cups watercress

1 tablespoon balsamic vinegar

pepper

- Heat 1 tablespoon of the oil in a 10 inch nonstick skillet and swirl around. Beat the eggs in a bowl with the basil and plenty of pepper, then pour into the pan in a thin layer and cook for 1–2 minutes until golden and set. Remove and cut into thick strips.

- Meanwhile, toss the feta and cherry tomatoes with the watercress in a serving bowl. Mix the remaining oil with the balsamic vinegar, pour over the salad, and toss to coat.

- Add the omelet strips, toss to mix, and serve while still warm.

 Cheese, Cherry Tomato, and Basil Frittata Heat 2 tablespoons olive oil in a 10 inch heavy skillet and swirl around. Beat 6 eggs in a pitcher and season well, then pour into the pan and cook over medium heat for 2–3 minutes. Sprinkle over 1 cup cherry tomatoes, halved, 7 oz feta cheese, drained and crumbled, and a handful of pitted black olives. Cook for an additional 3 minutes until the base is set, then place under a preheated high broiler, making sure that the pan handle is turned away from the heat, and cook for a further 2–3 minutes until the top is set and the feta has softened a little. Serve with a handful of arugula leaves and snipped basil leaves sprinkled over the top. Drizzle with lemon juice and serve in wedges.

 **Basil, Egg, and Cheese Pizza with Cherry Tomatoes** Make up a 5 oz package pizza base mix according to the package instructions and roll out to a 10 inch round on a large baking sheet. Spread with 8 tablespoons store-bought pizza topping sauce and sprinkle with ½ cup cherry tomatoes, halved, leaving a well in the center, then break an egg into the well. Sprinkle with a handful of basil leaves and ¾ cup ready-grated mozzarella cheese, avoiding the egg. Place in a preheated oven, 425°F, for 15–20 minutes until the base is browned and crisp and the cheese has melted.

Sweet Potato, Chickpea, and Cashew Curry

Serves 4

2 tablespoons vegetable oil

1 onion, chopped

4 sweet potatoes, peeled and chopped

3 tablespoons korma curry paste

13 oz can chickpeas, drained

13 oz can chopped tomatoes

1¾ cups canned coconut milk

⅔ cup toasted cashew nuts

3 tablespoons chopped fresh cilantro

warm naan breads or cooked rice, to serve (optional)

- Heat the oil in a large, deep, heavy skillet and cook the onion and sweet potatoes over medium heat, stirring occasionally, for 5 minutes until softened. Add the curry paste and cook, stirring, for 1 minute, then add the chickpeas, tomatoes, and coconut milk and bring to a boil.

- Reduce the heat and simmer for 10 minutes until the sauce has thickened slightly and the potatoes are tender. Stir in half the cashew nuts.

- Serve, garnished with the cilantro and remaining cashew nuts, with warm naan breads or cooked rice, if desired.

 Sweet Potato, Chickpea, and Cashew Couscous Add boiling water to a 7 oz package instant roasted vegetable–flavored couscous, following the package instructions, and allow to absorb the water for 5 minutes. Meanwhile, heat 2 tablespoons vegetable oil in a large, deep skillet and cook 1 chopped onion and 4 peeled and chopped sweet potatoes over medium heat, stirring occasionally, for 5 minutes until softened. Add a drained 13 oz can chickpeas and heat through. Stir into the couscous with 3 tablespoons chopped cilantro and ¾ cup toasted cashew nuts.

 Luxury Sweet Potato, Chickpea, and Cashew Korma In a food processor, whiz ⅓ cup whole blanched almonds with 2 garlic cloves until finely ground and like a paste. Heat 2 tablespoons vegetable oil in a large, deep skillet and cook 1 chopped onion with 4 peeled and chopped sweet potatoes and 3 tablespoons korma curry paste over medium heat, stirring occasionally, for 5 minutes until the vegetables are softened. Add the almond mixture and cook, stirring, for an additional 2 minutes, then add a 13 oz can chickpeas, drained, and a 13 oz can chopped tomatoes, 1 cup canned coconut milk and ½ cup heavy cream. Bring almost to a boil, then reduce the heat and simmer for 10 minutes until the sauce has thickened slightly and the potatoes are tender. Stir in ⅓ cup toasted cashew nuts. Serve sprinkled with 3 tablespoons chopped fresh cilantro and an extra ⅓ cup toasted cashew nuts, with warm naan breads or cooked rice, if desired.

30 Lemon Mixed Vegetable Kebabs with Nut Pilaff

Serves 4

1¼ cups easy-cook brown rice

1 eggplant, cut into chunks

2 zucchini cut into chunks

7 oz brown mushrooms, halved if large

4 tablespoons flat-leaf parsley, plus extra to serve

1 tablespoon rosemary leaves

⅔ cup olive oil

grated zest and juice of 2 lemons

1 cup cherry tomatoes

1 cup toasted slivered almonds

2 carrots, peeled and grated

2 tablespoons light soy sauce

salt and pepper

- For the pilaff, bring a large saucepan of lightly salted water to a boil and cook the rice for 25 minutes until tender. Drain and refresh under cold running water, then drain again.

- Meanwhile, place the eggplant, zucchini, and mushrooms in a large bowl. Chop the 4 tablespoons of parsley and the rosemary, and whisk together with the olive oil, lemon zest and juice in a bowl. Season with pepper, then pour over the vegetables and toss together.

- Thread the dressed vegetables with the tomatoes onto 8 metal skewers. Cook the skewers under a preheated medium broiler or over a barbecue, turning occasionally, for 8–10 minutes until lightly charred and tender.

- Toss the cooled rice with the almonds, carrots, the remaining parsley, and soy sauce. Season with a little pepper. Serve the hot kebabs on a bed of the rice salad.

 Egg-Fried Rice with Mixed Vegetables

Beat 2 eggs in a bowl. Heat 1 tablespoon vegetable oil in a large skillet, pour in the eggs in a thin layer, and cook over medium heat for 1–2 minutes until golden and set. Remove and shred. Heat another tablespoon of oil in the pan and stir-fry 10 oz frozen mixed stir-fry vegetables for 3–4 minutes. Add 2 cups ready-cooked long-grain rice and the shredded omelet and toss. Season with light soy sauce to taste and serve with ½ cup slivered almonds.

 Lemon Mixed Vegetable Kebabs with Minted Couscous

Prepare the vegetable kebabs as above. Place 1 cup couscous in a bowl and add enough boiling water to cover by ½ inch. Allow to absorb the water while cooking the kebabs as above. Whisk together 3 tablespoons olive oil, 2 tablespoons lemon juice, 1 tablespoon honey, ½ teaspoon harissa paste, and a handful of chopped mint in a bowl, then pour over the couscous and toss well to coat. Serve with the hot kebabs.

 # Mixed Mushroom Stroganoff

Serves 4

4 tablespoons olive oil
1 onion, finely chopped
12 oz brown mushrooms, trimmed
and quartered
6 oz shiitake mushrooms,
trimmed and halved
4 oz oyster mushrooms, trimmed
and halved
1 tablespoon brandy
1 teaspoon Dijon mustard
¾ cup sour cream pepper
cooked brown or white long-
grain rice, to serve
4 tablespoons chopped parsley

- Heat the oil in a large, heavy skillet and cook the onion over medium heat, stirring frequently, for 2–3 minutes until softened. Add the brown mushrooms and cook, stirring frequently, for 5 minutes until lightly browned. Add the shiitake and oyster mushrooms and cook, stirring frequently, for 5 minutes until softened.

- Pour the brandy into the mushroom mixture and stir over high heat until evaporated. Mix the mustard into the sour cream, then spoon into the pan and heat for 2 minutes until piping hot. Season well with pepper.

- Serve the stroganoff over cooked brown or white long-grain rice, with the parsley sprinkled over.

Mushroom Stroganoff on Whole-wheat Toast
Thickly slice 8 oz trimmed brown mushrooms and 8 oz trimmed portobello mushrooms. Melt 2 tablespoons garlic butter in a large skillet, add the mushrooms, and cook over high heat, stirring frequently, for 4–5 minutes. Meanwhile, toast and butter 4 thick slices of whole-wheat bread. Stir 1 tablespoon whole grain mustard and 1¼ cups sour cream into the mushrooms. Season to taste and serve on the toast with 1 tablespoon chopped chives sprinkled over.

 Pepper, Mustard, and Mushroom Stroganoff Melt 2 tablespoons butter in a large skillet with 2 teaspoons olive oil. Add 1 trimmed, cleaned, and thinly sliced leek and 1 red and 1 green cored, seeded, and sliced bell pepper and cook over medium heat, stirring occasionally, for 5 minutes. Add 12 oz trimmed and quartered chestnut mushrooms, 6 oz trimmed and halved shiitake mushrooms, and 4 oz trimmed and halved oyster mushrooms and cook, stirring frequently, for 3 minutes. Transfer to a plate. Add ⅔ cup dry white wine to the pan, bring to a boil, and continue boiling for 2–3 minutes until reduced by half. Meanwhile, stir 4 teaspoons whole grain mustard and 2 teaspoons prepared English mustard into 1¾ cups sour cream. Add to the pan and stir, then return the vegetables. Gently heat for 2 minutes, then stir in 4 tablespoons chopped flat-leaf parsley and season with pepper. Serve on a bed of cooked rice or with creamy mashed potato.

Quesadillas with Refried Beans and Avocado Salsa

Serves 4

1 tablespoon olive oil, plus extra
1 bunch of scallions, chopped
½ teaspoon ground cumin
½ teaspoon ground cilantro
½ teaspoon ground paprika
14¼ oz can refried beans
7 oz can red kidney beans,
    drained and rinsed
8 soft flour tortillas
1¾ cups grated cheddar cheese

For the salsa

2 vine-ripened tomatoes, chopped
1 ripe avocado, pitted, peeled,
    and roughly chopped
3 tablespoons chopped cilantro
1 tablespoon olive oil
pepper

- Heat the oil in a large, heavy skillet and cook the scallions over high heat, stirring frequently, for 2 minutes. Add all the spices and cook, stirring, for 1 minute. Add the refried beans and kidney beans and cook, stirring, for 2–3 minutes until piping hot, adding 2 tablespoons water to loosen if necessary.

- Divide the mixture between the flour tortillas. Fold each tortilla into quarters to encompass the filling, transfer to a lightly oiled ovenproof dish, and sprinkle with the cheddar.

- Cook under a preheated medium broiler for 5–10 minutes until the cheese has melted and the quesadillas are piping hot. Meanwhile, mix all the ingredients for the salsa together and season with pepper.

- Serve 2 quesadillas on each of 4 warmed serving plates and spoon over the salsa.

 Quick and Easy Quesadillas with Refried Beans Heat 1 tablespoon olive oil in a large, heavy skillet and cook 1 bunch of trimmed and roughly chopped scallions over high heat, stirring frequently, for 2 minutes. Add ½ teaspoon each ground cumin and cilantro and paprika, and cook, stirring, for 1 minute. Add a 14¼ oz can refried beans and cook, stirring, for 2–3 minutes until piping hot, adding 2 tablespoons water to loosen if necessary. Divide the bean mixture and ¾ cup grated cheddar cheese between 8 soft flour tortillas and add a spoonful of store-bought salsa to each. Fold each tortilla into quarters to encompass the filling, place on a foil-lined broiler rack, spaced apart, and sprinkle with another ¾ cup grated cheddar cheese. Warm under a preheated medium broiler for 2 minutes. Sprinkle with chopped cilantro to serve.

Quesadillas with Homemade Refried Beans Heat 2 tablespoons olive oil in a large skillet and cook 1 chopped onion and 1 roughly chopped small red chili over medium heat, stirring, for 5 minutes until softened. Add a drained 13 oz can cranberry beans and cook, stirring, for 2 minutes. Transfer to a food processor with a large handful of cilantro and blend but retaining some texture from the beans. Follow the recipe above, using the homemade refried beans in place of the canned refried beans.

30 Goat Cheese and Spinach Risotto

Serves 4

1 tablespoon olive oil
1 large onion, thinly sliced
1 garlic clove, chopped
1¼ cups Arborio risotto rice
3¾ cups hot vegetable stock
6 cups spinach leaves
finely grated zest and juice of
   1 lemon
6 oz rinded goat cheese, roughly
   chopped into cubes
pepper
freshly grated Parmesan cheese,
   to serve

- Heat the oil in a large, heavy skillet and cook the onion and garlic over medium heat, stirring occasionally, for 3–4 minutes until softened.

- Add the rice and cook, stirring, for 1 minute. Add half the stock and bring to a boil, then reduce the heat and simmer gently, stirring occasionally, for 5–6 minutes until almost all the stock has been absorbed. Add the remaining stock and continue simmering, stirring occasionally, until the rice is tender and almost all the stock has been absorbed. Add the spinach leaves and lemon zest and juice, and cook, stirring, for 2–3 minutes until the spinach has wilted and is well mixed through the rice.

- Sprinkle with the cheese and then stir through the risotto until almost melted yet still retaining some of its shape. Spoon into warmed serving bowls and serve with grated Parmesan and a good grinding of pepper.

---

10 Tagliatelle with Goat Cheese and Spinach Bring a large saucepan of lightly salted water to a boil and cook 1 lb fresh tagliatelle for 3–4 minutes or until just tender. Meanwhile, heat through 1¼ cups ready-made tomato pasta sauce in a saucepan. Drain the pasta and return to the pan. Toss in the sauce, add 6 cups spinach leaves, and stir over medium heat until the spinach wilts into the sauce. Serve with 4 oz goat cheese crumbled over the top and some freshly grated Parmesan cheese.

20 Goat Cheese and Spinach Pizza Spread each of 4 store-bought ready-made pizza bases with 1 tablespoon tomato paste. Heat a large saucepan over medium heat, add 6 cups spinach leaves, and heat until wilted, making sure that the spinach doesn't catch on the bottom of the pan. Arrange 6 oz rinded goat cheese, roughly chopped into cubes, and the spinach on the pizza bases, then grate 3 oz Parmesan cheese over the top. Drizzle with olive oil and place in a preheated oven, 400°F, for 10 minutes until the base is lightly browned. Serve with a green salad.

1 Tomato, Rosemary, and Cannellini Bean Stew

Serves 4

3 tablespoons olive oil

1 large red onion, sliced

2 teaspoons garlic paste

2 tablespoons chopped rosemary leaves

2 x 13 oz cans cannellini beans, drained

1 lb jar tomato pasta sauce

whole-wheat crusty bread, to serve

- Heat the oil in a large, heavy skillet and cook the onion over medium heat, stirring occasionally, for 2 minutes. Add the garlic paste and rosemary and cook, stirring constantly, for 30 seconds.

- Add the beans and tomato sauce and bring to a boil. Reduce the heat, cover, and simmer for 6–7 minutes until piping hot.

- Serve with fresh, torn whole-wheat bread for mopping up the juices.

 2 Vegetarian Navy Bean Cassoulet

Heat 3 tablespoons olive oil in a large, heavy skillet and cook 1 small chopped onion, 2 peeled and diced carrots, and 1 tablespoon chopped rosemary leaves over medium heat, stirring occasionally, for 3–4 minutes until softened. Add 2 x 13 oz cans navy beans, drained, with 2½ cups vegetable stock and bring to a boil. Simmer briskly, uncovered, for 10 minutes until piping hot, then place one-third of the beans into a food processor and whiz until smooth. Return the pureed beans to the pan, stir, and heat through briefly. Season with salt and pepper, then serve with crusty bread.

 3 Vegetarian Sausage and Lima Bean

Stew Heat 2 tablespoons olive oil in a large, deep, heavy skillet and cook 8 good-quality thick vegetarian sausages over medium heat, turning frequently, for 8–10 minutes until browned and cooked through. Add 2 red onions, cut into slim wedges, and cook, stirring frequently, for 5 minutes until softened. Add 2 x 13 oz cans each lima beans, drained, and chopped tomatoes with 4 tablespoons sundried tomato paste. Bring to a boil and simmer briskly, uncovered and stirring occasionally, for 10 minutes until the sauce is thick and pulpy. Serve in warmed serving bowls with plenty of chopped parsley sprinkled over.

30 Broiled Haloumi with Warm Couscous Salad

Serves 4

1 cup couscous
½ teaspoon salt
5 tablespoons olive oil
2 red onions, thinly sliced
1 red chili, roughly chopped
13 oz can chickpeas, drained
¾ cup cherry tomatoes, halved
3 tablespoons chopped parsley
1 tablespoon thyme leaves
12 oz haloumi cheese, thickly
   sliced

- Place the couscous in a bowl and add enough warm water to cover by ½ inch. Mix in the salt and allow the couscous to absorb the water for 20 minutes.

- Meanwhile, heat 3 tablespoons of the oil in a large skillet and cook the onions and two-thirds of the chili over medium heat, stirring, for 4–5 minutes until softened. Add the chickpeas and tomatoes and cook over high heat, stirring occasionally, for 3 minutes until the chickpeas are heated through and the tomatoes are softened but still retaining their shape.

- Meanwhile, mix the remaining olive oil and chili with the herbs in a shallow bowl. Add the haloumi slices and toss to coat. Place the haloumi slices on a broiler rack lined with foil and cook under a hot broiler for 2–3 minutes until browned in places.

- Stir the couscous into the chickpea mixture and cook for 1 minute to heat through. Serve piled onto warmed serving plates, topped with the haloumi slices.

 Quick Haloumi with Chili

Mix 2 chopped red chilies with 2 tablespoons extra virgin olive oil and allow to infuse while cooking the haloumi. Heat a nonstick skillet over high heat. Cut 12 oz haloumi cheese into medium slices. Cook the haloumi slices in batches for 2 minutes on each side until browned in places. When all the pieces are cooked, place a handful of salad leaves on each of 4 serving plates and top with the haloumi slices. Give the chili oil a stir, spoon it over the haloumi, and finish with a squeeze of lemon juice.

 Haloumi Cheese Kebabs with Couscous Place 1 cup couscous in a bowl and add enough warm water to cover by ½ inch. Mix in ½ teaspoon salt and allow to the couscous to swell and absorb the water for 20 minutes. Meanwhile, in a small bowl, mix together 3 tablespoons olive oil, 1 crushed garlic clove, 1 teaspoon each fresh thyme leaves and chopped oregano, rosemary, and mint, the juice of 1 lime, and salt and pepper. Place 12 oz haloumi cheese, cut into 1 inch cubes, and 8 trimmed brown mushrooms in a separate nonmetallic bowl, pour over the marinade, and mix to coat evenly. Cover and allow to marinate until you are ready to cook. Divide the cheese, mushrooms, and 8 cherry tomatoes evenly between 4 metal skewers, or bamboo skewers presoaked in cold water for 30 minutes. Cook over a barbecue or under a preheated high broiler for 5–6 minutes until tinged brown at the edges, brushing any remaining marinade over the kebabs while they cook. Serve the kebabs with store-bought salsa and the couscous.

Penne with Pan-Fried Butternut Squash and Pesto

Serves 4

1 lb fresh penne
2 tablespoons olive oil
2 tablespoons butter
1 lb ready-prepared butternut
 squash cubes or wedges
¾ cup green pesto
salt

- Bring a large saucepan of lightly salted water to a boil and cook the penne for 3 minutes or until just tender. Drain, return to the pan, and toss with 1 tablespoon of the olive oil.

- Meanwhile, melt the butter with the remaining tablespoon of oil in a large, heavy skillet or wok and cook the squash over medium heat, turning frequently, for 7–8 minutes until softened and golden, covering for the final 3 minutes of cooking to enable the steam to cook the squash.

- Add the pasta and pesto to the squash and toss all the ingredients together for 1 minute to heat through. Serve in warmed serving bowls.

Warm Butternut, Penne, Bacon, and Camembert Salad Cook the butternut squash as above. Meanwhile, cook 7 oz dried penne in a saucepan of salted boiling water for 10–12 minutes until just tender, then drain. Broil 8 slices bacon until browned and crisp. Snip into pieces, add to the squash with the pasta, and toss. Heat a skillet and cook ½ cup pine nuts over medium-high heat, shaking the pan, for 3–4 minutes until toasted. Place all the ingredients in a bowl with 4 cubed Camembert and 2½ cups mixed salad leaves. Whisk together 2 tablespoons olive oil, 1 tablespoon green pesto, and the juice of ½ lemon. Toss with the salad.

Summery Penne and Butternut Bake Bring a large saucepan of lightly salted water to a boil and cook 1 lb fresh penne for 3 minutes or until just tender. Drain, return to the pan, and toss with 1 tablespoon olive oil. Melt 2 tablespoons butter with 1 tablespoon olive oil in a large, heavy skillet or wok and cook 1 lb ready-prepared butternut squash cubes or wedges over medium heat, turning frequently, for 7–8 minutes until softened and golden, covering for the final 3 minutes and adding 1 ⅓ cup peas, defrosted if frozen, for the final 1 minute of cooking. Add 1 ¾ cups sour cream, the finely grated zest of 1 lemon, and 4 tablespoons green pesto and toss well, then crumble in 7 oz feta cheese and 4¼ cups baby spinach leaves. Heat, stirring, for 2 minutes until the sauce is hot and the spinach wilted. Toss with the pasta, pile into a large, shallow gratin dish, and sprinkle with 6 tablespoons freshly grated Parmesan cheese. Cook under a preheated high broiler for 3–4 minutes until golden and bubbling.

Ciabatta Toasties with Mediterranean Vegetables

Serves 4

5 tablespoons olive oil, plus extra
for drizzling
½ eggplant, trimmed and thinly
sliced
1 ciabatta loaf
4 tablespoons green pesto
1 large beef tomato, thinly sliced
4 slices of mozzarella cheese
pepper

· Heat the oil in a large, heavy skillet and cook the eggplant slices in batches over high heat for 1–2 minutes on each side until browned and tender. Remove with a fish spatula and keep warm.

· Meanwhile, cut the ciabatta loaf in half lengthwise, then each half in half again widthwise. Place on the broiler rack and cook under a preheated high broiler, cut-side up, for 1 minute until golden.

· Spread each ciabatta toastie with 1 tablespoon of the pesto. Top with the warm eggplant slices, then the tomato slices and finally the mozzarella slices. Drizzle each toastie with 1 tablespoon olive oil, then return to the broiler and cook for an additional 2 minutes until the mozzarella is melting and beginning to brown in places.

· Season with pepper and serve warm.

 Mediterranean Ciabatta Pizzas

Halve a ciabatta loaf lengthwise, then cut each half in half again widthwise. Place all 4 pieces on a baking sheet. Heat 4 tablespoons olive oil in a large, heavy skillet and cook ½ eggplant, trimmed and cut into cubes, over high heat, tossing frequently, for 5 minutes until browned and tender. Spread each of the ciabatta pieces with 2 tablespoons sundried tomato paste, then top with 1 sliced beef tomato. Divide the eggplant between the ciabatta pieces. Slice 5 oz mozzarella cheese and arrange over the top of the eggplant. Spoon 2 teaspoons green pesto over the top of each ciabatta piece, then cook under a preheated high broiler for 5 minutes until the tops are melted and golden.

 Mediterranean Vegetable Gratin

Heat 4 tablespoons olive oil in a large skillet and cook 1 sliced eggplant in batches over high heat for 1–2 minutes on each side until browned and tender. Loosely layer in a large, shallow gratin dish with 3 sliced large beef tomatoes, 10 oz mozzarella cheese, drained and thinly sliced, and 6 tablespoons green pesto, seasoning between the layers. Sprinkle with 3 tablespoons freshly grated Parmesan cheese and cook under a preheated high broiler for 8–10 minutes until golden and bubbling.

30 Fruity Chickpea Tagine with Cilantro Couscous

Serves 4

1 cup couscous

½ teaspoon salt

4 tablespoons olive oil

1 eggplant, cut into cubes

1 red onion, cut into chunks

2 red bell peppers, cut into chunks

1 tablespoon harissa paste

2 garlic cloves, chopped

1 inch piece of fresh ginger root, peeled and chopped

1 cinnamon stick

13 oz can chickpeas, drained

13 oz can chopped tomatoes

1¼ cups vegetable stock

1 tablespoon tomato paste

1 teaspoon sugar

⅔ cup ready-to-eat dried apricots, roughly chopped

⅓ cup ready-to-eat dried prunes, roughly chopped

4 tablespoons chopped fresh cilantro, plus extra to garnish

- Place the couscous in a bowl and add enough warm water to cover by ½ inch. Mix in the salt and allow the couscous to absorb the water while making the tagine.

- Heat 2 tablespoons of the oil in a large, heavy skillet and cook the eggplant over medium heat, stirring occasionally, for 5 minutes. Add the onion and red peppers and cook, stirring occasionally, for an additional 5 minutes. Stir in the harissa paste, garlic, and ginger and cook, stirring, for an additional 2 minutes. Add the cinnamon stick, chickpeas, tomatoes, stock, tomato paste, sugar, and dried fruit and bring to a boil. Reduce the heat, cover, and simmer for 10–15 minutes until all the vegetables are tender.

- Toss the couscous with the remaining 2 tablespoons oil, fluffing up with a fork. Stir in the chopped fresh cilantro. Serve with the tagine, sprinkling each plate with extra chopped fresh cilantro.

 Chickpea and Hummus Pita Pockets Lightly toast 4 pita breads. Cut each pita in half to form 2 pockets. Place 1 tablespoon store-bought chickpea hummus in each pocket together with 1 grated large carrot and ¼ chopped cucumber. Serve immediately.

 Chickpea, Tomato, and Feta Salad Finely slice 1 red onion and 2 red chiles, then toss with 1¼ cups roughly chopped tomatoes in a large salad bowl. Dress with the juice of 1½ lemons and about 6 tablespoons extra virgin olive oil. Season with salt and pepper. Warm through a drained 13 oz can chickpeas in a saucepan with 4 tablespoons water, then add about 90% to the bowl. Mash the remaining whole beans with a fork, then add to the bowl and toss all the ingredients to mix well. Allow to stand for the flavors to mingle for 5 minutes, then crumble over 7 oz feta cheese and sprinkle with some torn mint and basil leaves.

Spinach, Pine Nut, and Cheese Phyllo Pie

Serves 4

1 tablespoon olive oil

1 onion, roughly chopped

1 garlic clove, thinly sliced

½ cup pine nuts, toasted

2 lb frozen spinach, defrosted and well drained

2 eggs

2 egg yolks

14 oz feta cheese, drained and crumbled

2 teaspoons ground nutmeg

6 sheets of phyllo pastry, defrosted if frozen

2 tablespoons butter, melted

¼ cup freshly grated Parmesan cheese

salt and pepper

salad leaves dressed with olive oil and lemon juice, to serve

- Heat the oil in a large, heavy skillet and cook the onion and garlic over medium heat, stirring occasionally, for 5 minutes. Add the pine nuts and spinach and cook, stirring, for 3–4 minutes until heated through.

- Remove the pan from the heat and tip the mixture into a bowl. Add the whole eggs, egg yolks, feta, and nutmeg, stir well, and season with a little salt and plenty of pepper. Transfer to a large gratin dish.

- Crumple the sheets of phyllo pastry over the top, brush with the melted butter, and sprinkle with the Parmesan. Place in a preheated oven, 350°F, for 10–12 minutes until the pastry is golden and crisp.

- Serve hot with salad leaves dressed with olive oil and lemon juice.

 Spinach and Cheese Pesto Pasta

Bring a large saucepan of lightly salted water to a boil and cook 14 oz fresh spinach and ricotta tortellini for 2–3 minutes until just tender. Drain the pasta, return to the pan, and stir in 4 tablespoons green pesto. Serve in warmed bowls, sprinkled with Parmesan cheese shavings.

Spinach and Cheese Baked Eggs

In a bowl, mix together 2 lb defrosted and well-drained frozen spinach, 14 oz feta cheese, drained and crumbled, and 2 tablespoons whole-milk yogurt. Divide the mixture between 4 individual ramekins, then break an egg into each ramekin and season with salt and pepper. Top each ramekin with 1 tablespoon whole-milk yogurt. Place the ramekins in a baking pan and pour in enough boiling water to come halfway up the sides of the ramekins. Place on the center shelf of a preheated oven, 350°F, for 10 minutes. Serve immediately.

30 Vegetable, Fruit, and Nut Biryani

Serves 4

1¼ cups basmati rice

½ cauliflower, broken into florets

2 tablespoons vegetable oil

2 large sweet potatoes, peeled and cut into cubes

1 large onion, sliced

3 tablespoons hot curry paste

½ teaspoon ground turmeric

2 teaspoons mustard seeds

1¼ cups hot vegetable stock

2 cups fine green beans, topped and tailed and halved

⅔ cup golden raisins

6 tablespoons chopped cilantro

⅓ cup cashew nuts, lightly toasted

- Bring a large saucepan of lightly salted water to a boil and cook the rice for 5 minutes. Add the cauliflower and cook with the rice for an additional 10 minutes or until both are tender, then drain.

- Meanwhile, heat the oil in a large, heavy skillet and cook the sweet potatoes and onion over medium heat, stirring occasionally, for 10 minutes until browned and tender. Add the curry paste, turmeric, and mustard seeds and cook, stirring, for an additional 2 minutes.

- Pour in the stock and add the green beans. Bring to a boil, then reduce the heat and simmer for 5 minutes.

- Stir in the drained rice and cauliflower, raisins, cilantro and cashew nuts and simmer for another 2 minutes. Serve spooned onto warmed serving plates with pappadoms and raita.

10 Speedy Vegetable Curry with Rice

Cook ⅔ cup frozen cauliflower florets and 2 cups frozen green beans in a large saucepan of lightly salted water according to the package instructions. Drain and return to the pan, add 1¾ cups store-bought biryani curry sauce and heat through gently. Meanwhile, heat 3 cups ready-cooked pilau rice according to the package instructions. Serve the rice alongside the curry, sprinkled with lightly toasted cashew nuts, with pappadoms and raita.

20 Curried Vegetable Gratin

Melt 2 tablepoons butter in a large saucepan, add 3½ tablespoons all-purpose plain flour and cook over medium heat, stirring, for a few seconds. Remove from the heat and add 1¼ cups milk, a little at a time, stirring well between each addition. Stir in ½ cup grated cheddar cheese and ½ teaspoon curry powder. Return to the heat, then bring to a boil, stirring constantly, cooking until thickened. Add 1 lb mixed frozen vegetables, such as carrots, green beans, and cauliflower florets, and toss with the sauce. Divide between individual gratin dishes, then sprinkle with 2 tablespoons fresh white bread crumbs. Stand on a baking sheet and cook under a preheated high broiler for 8–10 minutes until browned and the vegetables are piping hot.

Vegetable Pad Thai

Serves 4

6 oz rice stick noodles

2 tablespoons sesame oil

2 eggs, beaten

1 tablespoon vegetable oil

2 cups bean sprouts

1 bunch of scallions, trimmed
and roughly chopped

1 teaspoon dried red pepper
flakes

1 tablespoon Thai fish sauce

1 tablespoon light brown sugar

⅓ cup salted peanuts, roughly
chopped

4 tablespoons chopped fresh
cilantro

lime wedges, to serve

- Place the rice noodles in a large heatproof bowl, cover with boiling water, and allow to soak for 10 minutes, or according to the package instructions, until tender. Drain and toss with 1 tablespoon of the sesame oil.

- Meanwhile, heat the remaining sesame oil in a large, heavy skillet, pour in the eggs in a thin layer, and cook over medium heat for 1–2 minutes until golden and set. Remove, shred, and add to the noodles.

- Heat the vegetable oil in the pan and stir-fry the bean sprouts and scallions over high heat for 2–3 minutes until softened, then add the red pepper flakes and stir well. Mix the fish sauce with the sugar and toss into the noodle mixture, then add to the pan with the peanuts and cook, tossing, for 2–4 minutes until piping hot.

- Serve in warmed serving bowls sprinkled with the cilantro, with lime wedges for squeezing over.

Instant Pad Thai Noodles Beat 2 eggs in a bowl. Heat 1 tablespoon sesame oil in a large, heavy skillet, pour in the eggs in a thin layer, and cook over medium heat for 1–2 minutes until golden and set. Remove, shred, and add to 12 oz ready-cooked rice noodles. Heat 1 tablespoon vegetable oil in the pan and stir-fry 2 cups bean sprouts and 1 bunch of trimmed and shredded scallions over high heat for 2–3 minutes until softened. Add the noodles and shredded omelet and ½ cup store-bought Pad Thai stir-fry sauce and toss until heated through. Sprinkle with some salted peanuts to serve.

Pad Thai-Style Sweet Potatoes and Sugar Snap Peas Heat 2 tablespoons vegetable oil in a large skillet and cook 1½ lb sweet potatoes, peeled and chopped, over medium heat, stirring, for 8–10 minutes until soft. Add 2½ cups sugar snap peas, 1 bunch of chopped scallions, 3 tablespoons light brown sugar, 2 tablespoons Thai fish sauce, and 1 teaspoon dried red pepper flakes and cook, stirring, for 6–8 minutes. Sprinkle with 1 cup chopped cilantro and ¾ cup roasted cashew nuts.

30 Chunky Vegetable Red Lentil Dahl

Serves 4

4 tablespoons vegetable oil
1 large onion, roughly chopped
1 eggplant, trimmed and roughly chopped
1 red bell pepper, cored, seeded, and cut into chunks
8 oz okra, trimmed and cut into 1 inch lengths
¾ cup split red lentils, rinsed
3 tablespoons balti curry paste
2½ cups vegetable stock
3 tablespoons chopped mint
¾ cup plain yogurt
5 tablespoons chopped fresh cilantro
salt and pepper
warm naan breads, to serve

- Heat the oil in a large, heavy saucepan and cook the onion and eggplant over medium heat, stirring occasionally, for 5 minutes, until softened and cooked through.

- Add the red pepper and okra to the pan and cook, stirring frequently, for 3–4 minutes before adding the lentils and curry paste. Stir well to mix, then pour in the stock. Bring to a boil, then reduce the heat, cover, and simmer for 20 minutes until the lentils are tender.

- Meanwhile, stir the mint into the yogurt.

- Remove the pan from the heat, stir in the cilantro and season with a little salt and pepper. Serve with the minted yogurt and warm naan breads.

---

10 Quick Red Lentil, Chunky Vegetable, and Chili Soup

Heat 2 tablespoons olive oil in a saucepan and cook 2 chopped onions, 1 finely chopped red chili, the finely grated zest of 1 lemon, and 1 teaspoon ground cumin over medium heat, stirring, for 2 minutes. Add 1 cup rinsed split red lentils, 7 oz frozen chunky mixed vegetables, and 3 cups hot vegetable stock, and simmer for 8 minutes until the lentils are tender. Stir through shredded mint and serve with plain yogurt and pita breads.

20 Chunky Vegetable Balti

Heat 4 tablespoons vegetable oil in a large saucepan and cook 1 large roughly chopped onion and 1 trimmed and roughly chopped eggplant over medium heat, stirring occasionally, for 5 minutes until softened and cooked through. Add 1 red bell pepper, cored, seeded, and cut into chunks, and 8 oz trimmed okra, cut into 1 inch lengths, and cook, stirring frequently, for 3–4 minutes. Stir in 3 tablespoons balti curry paste, then add 2½ cups vegetable stock.

Bring to a boil, then reduce the heat, cover, and simmer for 10 minutes. Meanwhile, prepare the minted yogurt as above. Serve with ready-cooked pilau rice, heated through according to the package instructions, and warm naan breads.

Rich Tomato and Chili Spaghetti

Serves 4

8 oz dried spaghetti
2 tablespoons olive oil
2 shallots, finely chopped
1 red chili, finely chopped
2 garlic cloves, thinly sliced
1 lb tomatoes, roughly chopped
3 tablespoons sundried
   tomato paste
⅔ cup red wine
6 tablespoons chopped parsley
salt and pepper
freshly grated Parmesan cheese,
   to serve (optional)

- Bring a large saucepan of lightly salted water to a boil and cook the spaghetti for 8–10 minutes until just tender. Drain, return to the pan, and toss with 1 tablespoon of the oil.

- Meanwhile, heat the remaining oil in a large, heavy skillet and cook the shallots, chili and garlic over medium heat, stirring frequently, for 2–3 minutes until slightly softened. Add the tomatoes, increase the heat, and cook, stirring occasionally, for 5 minutes until beginning to soften. Stir in the tomato paste and wine, cover, and simmer for 10 minutes until thick and pulpy.

- Stir in the parsley and season with pepper. Add the cooked spaghetti and toss well to coat in the sauce. Serve with freshly grated Parmesan, if desired.

 Easy Tomato, Chili, and Black Olive Spaghetti Bring a large saucepan of salted water to a boil and cook the spaghetti for 8–10 minutes until just tender. Drain, return to the pan, and toss with 1 tablespoon olive oil. Meanwhile, heat 2 tablespoons olive oil in a large skillet and cook 2 finely chopped shallots, 1 finely chopped red chili and 2 thinly sliced garlic cloves over medium heat, stirring, for 2–3 minutes until softened. Add a 2 cups red wine-flavoured ragu sauce and 1¼ cups pitted black olives, chopped, and heat through. Stir in 6 tablespoons chopped parsley, season with pepper, and serve with freshly grated Parmesan cheese.

 Roasted Eggplant and Tomato Spaghetti Bring a large saucepan of lightly salted water to a boil and cook 250 g (8 oz) dried spaghetti for 8–10 minutes until just tender. Drain, return to the pan and toss with 1 tablespoon olive oil. Meanwhile, trim and chop 1 eggplant into large chunks. Toss with 4 tablespoons olive oil in a roasting tin and place in a preheated oven, 220 °C (425 °F), Gas Mark 7, for 20 minutes. While the pasta and eggplant are cooking, heat 2 tablespoons olive oil in a large, heavy-based skillet and cook 2 finely chopped shallots, 1 finely chopped red chili and 2 thinly sliced garlic cloves over medium heat, stirring frequently, for 2–3 minutes until slightly softened. Add 1 lb tomatoes, increase the heat, and cook, stirring occasionally, for 5 minutes until beginning to soften. Stir in 3 tablespoons sundried tomato paste and ⅔ cup red wine, cover and simmer for 10 minutes until thick and pulpy, adding the roasted eggplant towards the end of the cooking time. Stir in 6 tablespoons chopped parsley and season with pepper. Add the spaghetti and toss well. Serve immediately.

30 Cauliflower and Potato Curry with Spinach

Serves 4

3 tablespoons vegetable oil
1 large onion, roughly chopped
1 cauliflower, trimmed and cut
into florets
1 lb potatoes, peeled and cut
into chunks
2 teaspoons cumin seeds
4 tablespoons korma curry paste
1¾ cups canned coconut milk
1¼ cups vegetable stock
6 cups spinach leaves
4 tablespoons chopped
fresh cilantro
salt and pepper
warm naan breads, to serve

- Heat the oil in a large, heavy saucepan and cook the onion over medium heat, stirring occasionally, for 2–3 minutes until beginning to soften, then add the cauliflower, potatoes, and cumin seeds. Cook for 4–5 minutes, stirring occasionally, until the potatoes are beginning to brown.

- Add the curry paste and toss to coat the vegetables, then stir in the coconut milk and stock and bring to a boil. Reduce the heat, cover, and simmer, stirring occasionally, for 20 minutes until the vegetables are tender, adding the spinach for the last 5 minutes of the cooking time.

- Season generously with salt and pepper and stir in the cilantro. Serve with warm naan breads.

 Cauliflower Thai Green Curry

Cook a 1 lb mixture of frozen cauliflower florets and green beans in a large saucepan of slightly salted boiling water according to the package instructions. Drain and return to the pan. Add a 1¾ cups Thai green curry sauce and heat through, stirring gently. Serve with ready-cooked Thai Jasmine rice, heated through according to the package instructions.

 Baked Cauliflower and Spinach Gratin

Trim 1 cauliflower, reserving a few inner leaves, and cut into florets. Place in a steamer with 2 torn bay leaves tucked among the florets and a few fresh gratings of nutmeg. Steam for 12 minutes until the cauliflower is tender. Meanwhile, rinse 6 cups spinach leaves, place in a large saucepan over medium heat, and stir gently until wilted. Squeeze out the excess moisture. Place the cauliflower and spinach in a large, greased gratin dish and pour over 1½ cups ready-made cheese sauce. Sprinkle over 2 cups fresh white bread crumbs and grate 2 oz Parmesan cheese on top. Place in a preheated oven, 400°F for 8 minutes until golden and bubbling. Serve with a green salad.

30 Butternut Squash, Tomato, and Red Onion Gratin

Serves 4

5 tablespoons butter
2 red onions, sliced
1½ lb butternut squash, peeled, seeded, and thinly sliced
2 tablespoons chopped parsley
3 tomatoes, thinly sliced
⅔ cup vegetable stock
3½ tablespoons plain flour
1¼ cup milk
½ teaspoon freshly grated nutmeg
1 teaspoon Dijon mustard
5 oz Emmental or Gruyère cheese, grated

To serve

crusty bread
salad

- Melt 3 tablepoons of the butter in a large, heavy skillet or wok and cook the onions and squash over medium-high heat, stirring occasionally, for 5 minutes until beginning to soften and brown in places. Add the parsley, tomatoes, and stock and bring to a boil. Reduce the heat, cover, and simmer for 5 minutes.

- Meanwhile, melt the remaining 2 tablespoons butter in a saucepan, add the flour, and cook over medium heat, stirring, for a few seconds. Remove from the heat and add the milk, a little at a time, stirring well between each addition. Return to the heat, then bring to a boil, stirring constantly, cooking until thickened. Remove from the heat, add the nutmeg, mustard, and half the cheese and stir well. Add to the pan with the squash and toss together.

- Transfer to a large gratin dish, sprinkle with the remaining cheese, and cook under a preheated medium broiler for 10 minutes until golden and bubbling. Serve with crusty bread and a simple salad.

---

10 Butternut, Sundried Tomato, and Red Onion Spaghetti

Cook 1 lb fresh spaghetti in a saucepan of lightly salted boiling water for 3–4 minutes or until just tender, then drain. Meanwhile, heat 1 tablespoon olive oil in a large, heavy skillet and cook 1 finely chopped red onion over medium heat, stirring frequently, for 5 minutes until softened. While the onion is cooking, cook 10 oz ready-prepared butternut squash in a microwave oven according to the package instructions, then add to the onion. Stir in 8 sundried tomatoes, drained and chopped, and 3 tablespoons balsamic vinegar, then add the drained pasta. Season and toss together with 2 handfuls of chopped basil and 7 oz feta cheese, drained and crumbled.

20 Butternut Squash, Tomato, and Red Onion Pasta

Melt 3½ tablespoons butter in a large skillet and cook 2 sliced red onions and 1½ lb thinly-sliced butternut squash over medium heat, stirring, for 5 minutes until soft and brown in places. Add 2 tablespoons chopped parsley, 3 sliced tomatoes, and ⅔ cup vegetable stock and bring to a boil. Cover and simmer for 5 minutes. Meanwhile, cook 8 oz dried fusilli according to the package instructions. Add to the sauce and toss together.

Coconut Dahl with Toasted Naan Fingers

Serves 4

1 tablespoon vegetable oil
1 onion, roughly chopped
2 tablespoons korma curry paste
⅔ cup split red lentils, rinsed
13 oz can coconut milk
naan breads, to serve

- Heat the oil in a heavy saucepan and cook the onion over high heat, stirring, for 1 minute, then stir in the curry paste and lentils. Pour in the coconut milk, then fill the can with water and add to the lentils. Simmer briskly, uncovered, for 8–9 minutes until the lentils are tender and the mixture is thick and pulpy.

- Meanwhile, lightly toast the naan breads under a preheated high broiler until warm and golden. Cut into fingers and serve alongside the dahl for dipping.

Coconut Dahl with Curried Onion

Naan Breads Make the dahl as above. Meanwhile, heat 2 tablespoons oil in a large, heavy skillet and cook 2 chopped onions and 1 chopped red onion over medium heat, stirring occasionally, for 5 minutes until softened. Add 8 tablespoons coconut milk, 3 tablespoons korma curry paste, 1 tablespoon mustard seeds, and 4½ cups spinach leaves and cook, stirring, for 2 minutes until the spinach has wilted. Lightly toast 2 naan breads on one side under a preheated medium broiler. Turn over, divide the onion mixture between the naan breads, and sprinkle with 4 tablespoons chopped fresh cilantro and 2 tablespoons shredded coconut. Lightly toast for 3–4 minutes until the coconut is golden. Serve each warm naan cut in half alongside the dahl.

Chunky Vegetable Dahl with Toasted

Naan Fingers Heat 4 tablespoons vegetable oil in a large saucepan and cook 1 roughly chopped onion, 1 trimmed and roughly chopped large zucchini and 1 trimmed and roughly chopped eggplant over medium-high heat, stirring occasionally, for 10 minutes until tender. Stir in 4 tablespoons korma curry paste and ⅓ cup rinsed split red lentils, then pour in 2½ cups vegetable stock and simmer for 10–15 minutes until thick and pulpy. Meanwhile, prepare the toasted naan fingers as above and serve with the dahl.

30 Puy Lentil Stew with Garlic and Herb Bread

Serves 4

4 tablespoons olive oil
1 red bell pepper, cut in chunks
1 green bell pepper, cut in chunks
1 red onion, roughly chopped
1 garlic clove, sliced
1 fennel bulb, trimmed and sliced
1¼ cups Puy lentils, rinsed
600 ml (1 pint) vegetable stock
300 ml (½ pint) red wine

For the garlic bread

3½ tablespoons butter, softened
1 garlic clove, crushed
2 tablespoons thyme leaves,
  roughly chopped
1 whole-wheat French baguette
salt and pepper

- Heat the oil in a large, heavy-based saucepan and cook the peppers, onion, garlic and fennel over a medium-high heat, stirring frequently, for 5 minutes until softened and lightly browned. Stir in the lentils, stock and wine and bring to a boil, then reduce the heat and simmer for 25 minutes until the lentils are tender.

- Meanwhile, beat the softened butter with the garlic and thyme in a bowl and season with a little salt and pepper. Cut the baguette into thick slices, almost all the way through but leaving the base attached. Spread the butter thickly over each slice, then wrap the baguette in foil and place in a preheated oven, 200°C (400°F), Gas Mark 6, for 15 minutes.

- Serve the stew hot, ladled into warm serving bowls, with the torn hot garlic and herb bread on the side for mopping up the juices.

 Chunky Tomato and Puy Lentil Soup

Heat 1 tablespoon olive oil in a large saucepan and cook 1 finely chopped onion over medium-high heat, stirring frequently, for 5 minutes. Add a 13 oz can chopped tomatoes, a drained 13 oz can Puy lentils, and 1 crushed garlic clove. Bring to a boil, then simmer for 4 minutes until warmed through. Season with salt and pepper. Divide between 4 warmed soup bowls and garnish each serving with 1 tablespoon sour cream and torn basil leaves. Serve with warm crusty bread.

 Puy Lentil and Sundried Tomato Salad Place 1 cup rinsed Puy lentils in a saucepan, cover generously with cold water, and bring to a boil. Reduce the heat and simmer for 15 minutes until just tender. Drain, then toss with the juice of 1 lemon, 1 crushed garlic clove, and 4 tablespoons olive oil, and season with salt and pepper. Stir a drained 9¼ oz jar sundried tomatoes, 1 small finely chopped red onion, and a handful of chopped flat-leaf parsley through the lentils and serve with some arugula leaves.

QuickCook

Fuss-Free
Family
Desserts

Recipes listed by cooking time

10

Gingered Apricots with Mascarpone and Brioche

Serves 4

2 tablespoons butter

12 oz apricots, pitted and quartered

4 tablespoons light brown sugar

6 tablespoons stem ginger syrup

2 pieces of stem ginger, finely chopped

1 cup mascarpone cheese

2 tablespoons Demerara sugar

toasted slices of brioche, to serve

- Melt the butter in a heavy skillet and cook the apricots over medium heat, stirring occasionally, for 3–4 minutes until soft and browned in places. Sprinkle with the brown sugar and cook, stirring, for 1 minute. Add the stem ginger syrup, stir well, and cook for 1 minute more, then remove from the heat.

- Mix the stem ginger with the mascarpone and Demerara sugar.

- Serve the apricots on warm toasted brioche with a spoonful of the ginger cream on top, allowing it to melt.

 Quick Gingered Apricots with Amaretti Melt 25 g (1 oz) butter in a heavy-based saucepan and cook a well-drained 400 g (13 oz) can halved apricots over a high heat, stirring, for 2–3 minutes. Sprinkle over 50 g (2 oz) soft light brown sugar and cook for 2–3 minutes, allowing the sugar to caramelize slightly. Pour over 2 tablespoons orange juice and heat for 1 minute, then transfer to a warmed serving dish and scatter over 8 lightly crushed amaretti biscuits. Serve with Greek yogurt.

 Gingered Nectarines and Peaches Heat ½ cup superfine sugar, a 1½ inch piece of fresh ginger root, peeled and grated, and 1¾ cups pomegranate juice in a heavy-based saucepan for 2 minutes until the sugar has dissolved. Bring to a boil, then simmer for 10 minutes until reduced to a syrup. Pit 4 nectarines and 4 peaches. Cut each nectarine into 8 wedges and each peach into quarters. Add to the hot syrup and allow to cool slightly, then add 1½ cups fresh raspberries. Stir through 2 pieces of chopped stem ginger and serve with whole milk yogurt.

FAM-DESS-WES

30 Chocolate and Raspberry Layers

Serves 4

7 oz bittersweet chocolate,
   broken into pieces
1¼ cups heavy cream
2 cups fresh raspberries
unsweetened cocoa powder,
   for dusting
mint sprigs, to decorate
   (optional)

- Place the chocolate in a heatproof bowl and set over a saucepan of gently simmering water. Stir until melted and smooth, then remove from the heat. Line 2 baking sheets with parchment paper and spoon 12 x 4 inch rounds of melted chocolate onto the paper. Refrigerate or freeze for 15 minutes until firm and set.

- Meanwhile, whip the cream in a bowl until soft peaks form. Place the raspberries in a bowl and very lightly mash with a fork until lightly crushed and juicy. Fold the crushed raspberries into the whipped cream.

- Carefully peel the disks of chocolate away from the paper. Place a chocolate disk on each of 4 chilled dessert plates, top with half the raspberry cream, and add another chocolate disk to each stack. Top with the remaining raspberry cream and chocolate disks. Dust a little cocoa powder over each stack and decorate with a mint sprig, if desired.

 Speedy and Naughty Raspberry Ice Cream Sundae Place 7 oz white chocolate, broken into pieces, in a heatproof bowl and set over a saucepan of gently simmering water. Stir until melted and smooth, then remove from the heat. Meanwhile, in each of 4 serving glasses place 1 scoop vanilla ice cream, followed by 1 scoop raspberry ice cream and then another scoop of vanilla ice cream. Sprinkle with some fresh raspberries and pour over the melted white chocolate. Serve immediately.

 Raspberry Fool Place 2 cups fresh raspberries in a skillet and lightly crush with a fork. Add ¾ cup superfine sugar and 2 teaspoons lemon juice and cook over medium-low heat, stirring gently, until the sugar has dissolved. Simmer for 3 minutes until the raspberries are soft and the juices are syrupy, then allow to cool. Whip 1¼ cups heavy cream in a bowl until soft peaks form. Fold through the raspberry mixture with 1 cup whole fresh raspberries. Spoon into serving glasses.

Make-Ahead Cheesecakes with Berry Compote

Serves 4

8 gingersnap cookies
2 tablespoons butter, melted
1¾ cups cream cheese
⅓ cup superfine sugar
finely grated zest and juice
   of 1 lime
3 tablespoons light cream
¾ cup fresh raspberries
¾ cup fresh blueberries
2 tablespoons grenadine

· Place the cookies in a plastic bag and bash with a rolling pin to form fine crumbs. Tip into a saucepan or bowl with the melted butter and mix well. Divide between 4 individual ramekins and press to form a firm base. Refrigerate while making the topping.

· Beat together the cream cheese, sugar, and lime zest and juice in a bowl until smooth. Fold in the cream, then spoon over the cheesecake bases and roughly spread. Refrigerate for 5–10 minutes while making the compote.

· In a separate bowl, gently mix the berries with the grenadine.

· Serve the cheesecakes with the berry compote spooned on top in the center.

 Mini Berry Cheesecake Tartlets Beat 4 tablespoons lemon curd into 1¾ cups cream cheese. Pour 1 teaspoon summer fruit sauce from a jar into each of 8 store-bought ready-made sweet dessert tartlet cases. Top with a spoonful of the cheese mixture and then sprinkle with 2 cups mixed fresh berries. Serve with a sifting of confectioners' sugar.

 Raspberry Cheesecake with Raspberry Liqueur Place 5 oz graham crackers in a plastic bag and bash with a rolling pin to form fine crumbs. Mix with ¼ cup toasted slivered almonds and 5 tablespoons melted butter in a bowl. Press into an 8 inch removable-bottomed tart pan and refrigerate. Beat together 1¾ cups cream cheese, ⅓ cup superfine sugar, and the zest and juice of 1 lemon. Fold in ⅔ cup heavy cream, then spread over the crumb base and refrigerate until ready to serve. Make a raspberry compote by warming 2½ cups fresh raspberries with 2 tablespoons confectioners' sugar in a saucepan. Crush lightly with a fork. Add 2–3 tablespoons crème de framboise liqueur and stir. Spoon on top of the cheesecake before serving.

2 ⏱ Pear and Chocolate Crumble

Serves 4

3 x 13½ oz cans pears, drained

5 tablespoons dark brown sugar

2 cups all-purpose flour

17 tablespoons butter at room
temperature, cut into cubes

½ cup Demerara sugar

4 oz milk chocolate, very roughly
chopped

1 tablespoon custard powder

2 tablespoons unsweetened
cocoa powder

1 tablespoon superfine sugar

1¼ cup milk

- Roughly chop the pears and place in a bowl, add the brown sugar, and toss well to coat. Transfer to a large gratin dish.

- Place the flour and butter in a food processor and pulse until coarse bread crumbs form. Transfer to a bowl and stir in the Demerara sugar and chocolate.

- Sprinkle the crumble mixture over the top of the pears and place in a preheated oven, 425°F, for 10–12 minutes until just beginning to brown.

- Meanwhile, place the custard powder, cocoa, and superfine sugar in a heatproof bowl and blend to a paste with about 1 tablespoon of the milk. Heat the remaining milk in a saucepan until almost boiling, then pour onto the custard powder mixture, stirring constantly. Return the mixture to the pan and bring to a boil over gentle heat, stirring constantly, until thickened.

- Serve the crumble hot with the chocolate custard.

 Pan-Fried Pears with Chocolate Sauce Drain 3 x 410 g (13½ oz) cans pears and cut each in half. Melt 25 g (1 oz) unsalted butter in a large saucepan and cook the pears over a high heat, stirring frequently, for 2 minutes. Stir in 1 tablespoon soft light brown sugar and cook for a further minute. Add 75 g (3 oz) roughly chopped plain dark chocolate and 2 tablespoons double cream. Reduce the heat to low and stir constantly until the chocolate has melted and the sauce becomes glossy and smooth. Serve warm.

 Chewy Chocolate and Pear Cookies Place 2 cups all-purpose flour and 7 tablespoons butter at room temperature, cut into cubes, in a food processor and pulse until coarse bread crumbs form. Add 1 egg and process briefly to mix, then add 4 oz very roughly chopped milk chocolate and 1 peeled, cored, and chopped small pear and process again briefly. Form into 15 balls, then press onto a lightly greased baking sheet, using a fork to flatten them a little. Bake in a preheated oven, 425°F, for 12 minutes until just beginning to brown. Serve slightly warm.

10 Raspberry Rice Brûlée

Serves 4

⅔ cup fresh raspberries
1 tablespoon suprefine sugar
1 tablespoon water
14 oz can rice pudding
4 tablespoons heavycream
⅔ cup light brown sugar

· Place the raspberries in a saucepan with the superfine sugar and measurement water and heat gently for 2 minutes until the raspberries are slightly softenened. Divide between 4 individual ramekins.

· Gently heat the rice pudding and cream in a separate saucepan for 2 minutes until hot. Spoon the rice mixture over the raspberries, then top with a thick layer of the brown sugar and level.

· Stand the ramekins on a baking sheet and cook under a preheated high broiler for 1–2 minutes until the sugar caramelizes and becomes crisp. Serve warm.

2 Traditional Crème Brûlée

with Raspberries Place ⅔ cup fresh raspberries in a saucepan with 1 tablespoon each superfine sugar and water, and heat gently for 2 minutes until the raspberries are slightly softened. Divide between 4 individual ramekins. Bring 1¼ cups milk to a boil. Meanwhile, beat together 2 egg yolks, 4 tablespoons each superfine sugar and heavy cream and 1 tablespoon cornstarch in a heatproof bowl. Pour over the hot milk, stirring constantly, then return the mixture to the rinsed-out pan and gently heat, stirring constantly, until a thick custard is formed. Pour over the raspberries in the ramekins. Sprinkle with ⅔ cup light brown sugar. Using a kitchen blowtorch, cook the sugar until it has caramelized. Serve warm.

3 Vanilla Rice Pudding with Raspberry Compote

Place 1¼ cups Arborio risotto rice in a saucepan with 2½ cups milk, 1¼ cups heavy cream and 1 vanilla bean, split lengthwise. Bring to a boil and add ⅔ cup soft light brown sugar. Reduce the heat, cover, and simmer for 20–25 minutes until the rice is tender. Meanwhile, place 1½ cups raspberries in a saucepan with ¼ cup superfine sugar and 1 tablespoon water. Heat gently, stirring occasionally, for 2–3 minutes until the sugar dissolves and the fruit is soft and warm. Remove the vanilla bean from the rice and serve the rice pudding in warmed serving bowls, with the compote spooned on top.

White Chocolate Cream with Raspberries

Serves 4

5 oz white chocolate, broken into pieces, plus extra shavings to decorate

1½ cups heavy cream

¾ cup sour cream

1 cup fresh raspberries, lightly mashed

bittersweet chocolate shavings, to decorate

- Place the white chocolate in a saucepan with 8 tablespoons of the cream and gently heat, stirring constantly, until the chocolate has melted and the mixture is smooth. Remove from the heat.

- Place the remaining cream in a plastic bowl and whisk until soft peaks form. Fold in thesour cream, then fold in the warm chocolate mixture. Finally, fold in the raspberries. Freeze in the bowl for 5 minutes.

- Divide the mixture between 4 serving glasses and decorate with white and bittersweet chocolate shavings.

 Chunky Chocolate Cream with Raspberries Whip 1¼ cups heavy cream until soft peaks form. Roughly chop 6 oz white chocolate and sprinkle over the whipped cream. Lightly crush ¾ cup fresh raspberries with a fork on a plate, then fold into the cream with the chocolate until marbled. Spoon into 4 serving glasses.

 Rum Cream with Strawberries In a food processor, whizz 2⅔ cups hulled strawberries (reserving a few for decoration) with ¼ cup superfine sugar until pureed, then refrigerate. Whip ⅔ cup heavy cream in a bowl until slightly thickened, then fold in 2 tablespoons superfine sugar, 1 tablespoon dark rum, and ½ teaspoon vanilla extract. In each of 4 serving glasses make alternate layers of the strawberry puree and cream mixture, finishing with the cream. Refrigerate until ready to serve. Decorate with the reserved strawberries and serve with store-bought shortbread cookies, if desired.

3⦿ Warm Spiced Plums with Ice Cream

Serves 4

1½ lb ripe plums, halved
  and pitted
½ cup superfine sugar
½ teaspoon ground cinnamon
½ teaspoon ground ginger
3 tablespoons water
good-quality ice cream, to serve

- Place all the ingredients except the ice cream in a large, heavy saucepan and bring to a boil, stirring occasionally. Reduce the heat to low, cover, and very gently simmer, stirring occasionally, for 15–20 minutes until the plums are tender.

- Transfer to a large serving dish and allow to cool for 5 minutes before serving.

- Serve with scoops of good-quality ice cream.

1⦿ Caramelized Plums, Apricots, and Peaches Halve and pit a 1½ lb mixture of ripe plums, apricots, and peaches. Heat a large, nonstick skillet over medium heat. Press the cut side of each fruit half into a plate of sugar (any variety) and cook, sugar-side down, for 3–5 minutes or until the sugar has melted and turned golden. Allow to cool slightly, then serve with thick whole-milk yogurt drizzled with honey.

2⦿ Plums with Honey and Mascarpone Pit and slice 2 plums and 2 apricots and place in a serving bowl. Peel and slice 1 kiwifruit and pit and slice 1 cup cherries. Add to the bowl with the plums and apricots and gently mix together. Mix 1 cup mascarpone cheese with 2 tablespoons honey, ½ teaspoon vanilla extract, and the seeds from 1 vanilla bean in a separate bowl. Spoon the fruit into dishes and serve the mascarpone mixture on the side.

30 Apricots with Lemon Cream and Soft Amaretti

Serves 4

1 lb apricots, halved and pitted
4 tablespoons light brown sugar
1 vanilla bean, split lengthwise
5 tablespoons water
finely grated zest of 1 lemon
¾ cup sour cream

For the amaretti

1 egg white
⅔ cup ground almonds
¼ cup superfine sugar

- Place the apricots in a heavy saucepan with the brown sugar, vanilla bean and the measurement of water and bring to a boil. Reduce the heat, cover, and simmer for 15 minutes until the apricots are tender yet just retaining their shape.

- Meanwhile, for the amaretti, whisk the egg white in a grease-free bowl until stiff. Fold in the ground almonds and superfine sugar until well mixed. Line a baking sheet with parchment paper and spoon tablespoonfuls of the mixture onto the lined sheet, well spaced apart.

- Bake in a preheated oven, 375°F, for 10 minutes until just beginning to brown. Allow to cool on the paper for 5 minutes, then carefully peel away from the paper and transfer to a cooling rack.

- Mix the lemon zest into the sour cream. Remove the vanilla bean from the apricots and spoon the apricots into serving dishes. Serve with the lemon cream and soft amaretti.

10 Apricot and Peach Pavlovas Spoon 2 tablespoons extra-thick heavy cream into each of 4 store-bought ready-made meringue nests. Drain 13 oz canned apricots, thinly slice, and arrange on top of the cream. Decorate each pavlova with a mint sprig.

20 Apricot and Hot Cross Bun Pudding Cut 4 store-bought hot cross buns into chunks and place them in a greased ovenproof dish. Spoon 6 tablespoons apricot jelly over the hot cross buns and pour 1¾ cups ready-to-serve custard over the top. Place in a preheated oven, 350°F, for 10–15 minutes until bubbling hot. Serve immediately.

1 Eggy Fruit Bread with Berries and Cream

Serves 4

2 eggs

4 tablespoons milk

2 tablespoons superfine sugar

½ teaspoon ground cinnamon

2 tablespoons butter

4 thick slices of fruit bread

1 cup mixed fresh berries

8 tablespoons sour cream

confectioners' sugar, for dusting

maple syrup, for drizzling

- Beat the eggs with the milk, superfine sugar and cinnamon in a bowl. Melt the butter in a large, heavy skillet. Dip the fruit bread slices, 2 at a time, into the egg mixture on both sides and allow to soak in the mixture, then lift out and cook over medium heat for 1–2 minutes on each side until golden and set. Remove and stack to keep warm.

- Meanwhile, mix half the berries into the sour cream.

- Spoon the berry cream onto the warm toasts, then sprinkle with the remaining berries and dust with confectioners' sugar. Drizzle with maple syrup and serve.

 Eggy Chocolate Bread with Raspberries Beat 2 eggs with 4 tablespoons good-quality store-bought chocolate milkshake, 2 tablespoons superfine sugar and ½ teaspoon ground cinnamon in a bowl. Melt 2 tablespoons butter in a large, heavy skillet. Dip 4 thick slices of brioche, 2 at a time, into the egg mixture on both sides and allow to soak in the mixture, then lift out and cook over medium heat for 1–2 minutes on each side until golden and set. Remove and stack to keep warm. Place 4 oz chopped bittersweet chocolate in a saucepan with 6 tablespoons heavy cream and 1 tablepoon butter. Heat gently, stirring constantly, until the sauce is smooth and melted. Serve the chocolate breads topped with spoonfuls of extra-thick heavy cream, sprinkled with ¾ cup fresh raspberries and 2 oz roughly chopped bittersweet chocolate, then drizzled with the warm chocolate sauce.

Berry Bread and Butter Pudding Lightly butter 8 slices of fruit bread and layer in a large, shallow gratin dish with 1 cup mixed berries, defrosted if frozen. Beat together 3 eggs, 2 cups milk, ¼ cup superfine sugar, and ½ teaspoon ground cinnamon in a bowl, then pour over the bread and berries. Place in a preheated oven, 400°F, for 20 minutes until lightly set and golden. Sprinkle with 2 tablespoons Demerara sugar to serve.

3○ Chocolate Mousse with Pistachio Ice Cream

Serves 6

7 oz bar bittersweet chocolate,
  broken into pieces
14 tablespoons unsalted butter,
  cut into cubes
3 eggs
⅓ cup superfine sugar
confectioners' sugar, for dusting
pistachio or vanilla ice cream,
  to serve

- Place the chocolate and butter in a heatproof bowl and set over a saucepan of gently simmering water. Stir until melted and smooth, then remove from the heat.

- Whisk the eggs and sugar together in a large bowl until pale and thick, then fold in the melted chocolate and butter until well mixed.

- Divide between 6 individual ramekins and place on a baking sheet. Bake in a preheated oven, 300°F , for 7 minutes until just firm.

- Allow to cool for 10 minutes, then dust with confectioners' sugar and serve with a scoop of pistachio or vanilla ice cream on top of each mousse.

1○ Coffee-Drowned Ice Cream with Chocolate Liqueur Place small scoops of vanilla ice cream in the bottom of 6 small glasses. Pour over a little chilled chocolate liqueur and top with a shot of freshly made espresso coffee. Serve immediately.

2○ Bananas and Ice Cream with Rich Chocolate Sauce Place 3½ tablespoons butter, ½ cup unsweetened cocoa powder, and ¼ cup each light brown sugar and superfine sugar in a saucepan. Add ¾ cup milk and ½ teaspoon vanilla extract. Heat gently over medium heat, stirring, until smooth. Bring to a boil, then simmer until the sauce has thickened. Slice 1 banana into each of 6 serving glasses, add scoops of vanilla ice cream to each, and pour over the sauce.

Banoffee Layers

Serves 4

6 graham crackers
2 large bananas
3½ tablespoons butter
¼ cup dark brown sugar
¾ cup heavy cream
⅔ cup sour cream
grated bittersweet chocolate,
  to decorate

- Place the carckers in a plastic bag and bash with a rolling pin to form fine crumbs. Divide between 4 tall serving glasses and use to line each base.

- Mash one of the bananas and divide between the 4 glasses, spooning on top of the cracker crumbs.

- Melt the butter in a small saucepan, add the sugar, and heat over medium heat, stirring well, until the sugar has dissolved. Add the cream and cook gently for 1–2 minutes until the mixture is thick. Remove from the heat and allow to cool for 1 minute, then spoon on top of the mashed banana.

- Slice the second banana and arrange on top of the caramel, then spoon over the sour cream. Decorate with grated bittersweet chocolate before serving.

 Banoffee and Date Pudding

Lightly whip 1¼ cups heavy cream in a large bowl. Crumble in 4 store-bought ready-made meringue nests, then fold in 4 sliced bananas and a handful of chopped pitted dates. Swirl over 4 tablespoons store-bought toffee sauce. Spoon into 4 serving dishes, sprinkle with a handful of pecan nuts, and drizzle with a little more toffee sauce.

 Quick-Fix Banoffee Pie

Line an 8 inch tart pan with plastic wrap. In a food processor, whiz together 1 cup pitted dates and 1½ cups whole blanched almonds. Press into the tart pan and freeze for 10 minutes. Place 1¼ cups whole-milk yogurt in a wide, shallow dish and sprinkle with 2 tablespoons dark brown sugar, then refrigerate for 5 minutes. Transfer to a serving plate, peeling away the plastic wrap. Sprinkle with 2 sliced bananas. Swirl the sugar into the yogurt and spoon over, retaining the ripple effect. Finish with a grating of bittersweet chocolate and serve immediately.

30 Oat-Topped Orchard Fruit Crumbles

Serves 4

4 cooking apples, peeled, cored, and roughly chopped
2 tablespoons light brown sugar
2 tablespoons superfine sugar
3 tablespoons water
1 cup blackberries
¾ cup all-purpose flour
5 tablespoons unsalted butter, cut into cubes
1 cup rolled oats
½ cup Demerara sugar
½ teaspoon ground cinnamon
ice cream, clotted cream, or sour cream, to serve

· Place the apples, brown sugar, superfine sugar, and measurement water in a heavy saucepan and cook over gentle heat, stirring occasionally, for 5–8 minutes until the apples are soft and just beginning to turn pulpy. Fold in the blackberries, cover, and remove from the heat. Keep warm.

· Place the flour in a large bowl, add the butter, and blend in with the fingertips until the mixture resembles coarse bread crumbs. Stir in the oats, Demerara sugar, and cinnamon. Spread out in a large roasting pan and place in a preheated oven, 400°F, for 10–15 minutes, stirring halfway through cooking, until golden.

· Spoon the warm fruit into warmed serving bowls and top with the warm golden crumble. Serve with ice cream, clotted cream, or sour cream.

10 Quick Orchard-Fruit Compote Pudding Drain a 13 oz can or jar apples or pears and roughly chop. Place in a saucepan with 3 tablespoons light brown sugar and cook over medium heat, stirring occasionally, for 3–4 minutes. Divide 1¼ cups whole-milk yogurt between 4 glass bowls. Swirl through the warm fruit compote and serve with store-bought shortbread.

20 Mixed Summer Fruit Crumbles Divide 2 cups frozen mixed summer fruits between 4 ramekins. Sprinkle 2 teaspoons vanilla sugar and 1 teaspoon cornstarch over each ramekin and stir around a little. Cover each with 1–2 tablespoons store-bought ready-made crumble mix. Stand the ramekins on a baking sheet and place in a preheated oven, 425°F, for 15 minutes. Serve with vanilla ice cream.

Pan-Fried Pineapple with Rum and Raisins

Serves 4

½ pineapple, skinned, cored,
and cut into thin slices
2 tablespoons unsalted butter
2 tablespoons dark brown sugar
4 tablespoons dark rum
4 tablespoons raisins
ice cream, to serve

- Halve each of the pineapple slices. Melt the butter in a large, heavy skillet and cook the pineapple slices over high heat for 2–3 minutes on each side until golden and softened. Sprinkle with the sugar, toss, and cook for 1 minute, then pour in the rum and sprinkle with the raisins. Cook, tossing, for an additional 2 minutes until heated through.

- Divide between 4 serving bowls and add a large scoop of vanilla ice cream to each serving.

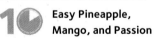 **Easy Pineapple, Mango, and Passion Fruit Pan-Fry** Melt 2 tablespoons butter in a large skillet and cook 14 oz prepared mixed fresh pineapple, mango, and passion fruit over high heat, turning frequently, for 3–4 minutes. Sprinkle with 2 tablespoons light brown sugar and 1 teaspoon apple-pie spice. Cook, tossing, for an additional 2 minutes. Serve immediately with pouring cream.

Pineapple Flambé Skin and slice 1 pineapple, then remove the cores with an apple corer. Melt 3½ tablespoons butter in a large frying pan and cook the pineapple slices in a single layer in batches for 90 seconds on each side. Transfer to a bowl. Add the seeds from 1 vanilla pod, 50 g (2 oz) light muscovado sugar and the juice of 1 orange to the pan and cook, stirring, until the sugar has dissolved.

Return the cooked pineapple and any juices to the pan and cook until piping hot. Pour over 3 tablespoons dark rum and set alight. Remove from the heat and allow the flames to die down, then serve with pouring cream.

3. Rhubarb and Ginger Tartlets

Serves 4

6oz prepared sweet shortcrust
   pastry, defrosted if frozen
all-purpose flour, for dusting
1 lb rhubarb, trimmed and cut
   into chunks
¼ cup superfine sugar
3 pieces of stem ginger, chopped
pinch of ground ginger
2 tablespoons stem ginger syrup
1 tablespoon unsalted butter
ice cream or sour cream, to serve

- Roll out the pastry on a lightly floured work surface and use to line 4 x 4 inch fluted tartlet pans. Prick the base of each a few times with a fork.

- Line each tartlet shell with a piece of scrunched parchment paper and fill with pie weights. Place in a preheated oven, 400°F, for 15 minutes, then remove the paper and weights and bake for an additional 2–3 minutes.

- Meanwhile, place the rhubarb in a heavy saucepan with all the remaining ingredients except the ice cream or sour cream and cook over medium heat, stirring occasionally, for 5 minutes. Reduce the heat and simmer gently, stirring occasionally, for 10 minutes until the rhubarb is tender and pulpy.

- Remove the tartlet shells from their pans. Place each on a serving plate and fill with the rhubarb mixture. Serve warm with ice cream or sour cream.

---

1. Rhubarb and Ginger Compote Cut 1 lb trimmed rhubarb into ¼ inch slices. Place in a saucepan with ¾ cup superfine sugar, 3 pieces of finely chopped stem ginger, and 2 teaspoons vanilla extract and bring to a boil, stirring to help dissolve the sugar. Partially cover and simmer for about 3 minutes, then uncover and cook for an additional 2 minutes until the rhubarb is tender. Pour into a bowl and allow to cool a little until you are ready to serve with either vanilla ice cream or custard.

2. Rhubarb and Ginger Trifle
Place 6 trimmed and roughly chopped rhubarb sticks in a saucepan with 6 tablespoons water and ¾ cup superfine sugar and cook over medium heat, stirring frequently, for 5 minutes. Strain, reserving the liquid, and allow to cool for 5 minutes. Stir 2 tablespoons Grand Marnier into the rhubarb liquid. Whip together 1 cup mascarpone cheese, ½ cup whole-milk yogurt and ½ cup confectioners' sugar in a bowl until thickened.

Slice ½ store-bought Jamaican ginger cake into 8 pieces. Place a slice of cake in the bottom of each of 4 wine glasses, then drizzle each with enough rhubarb liquid to moisten the cake. Add a spoonful of rhubarb to each glass, top with another slice of cake, and drizzle each with a little more rhubarb liquid. Top with the remaining rhubarb. Divide the mascarpone mixture between the glasses and sprinkle with toasted slivered almonds and chopped stem ginger.

30 Warm Creamy Coconut Rice with Mango and Lime

Serves 4

½ cup Arborio risotto rice
⅓ cup superfine sugar
1¼ cups milk
1¾ cups canned coconut milk
½ mango, pitted, peeled and
  cut into small chunks
finely grated zest and juice
  of 1 lime

- Place the rice in a heavy saucepan with the sugar, milk, and coconut milk. Bring to a boil, then reduce the heat and simmer for 20 minutes until the rice has swelled and thickened.

- Meanwhile, place the mango in a bowl and mix with the lime zest and juice.

- Spoon the cooked rice into serving bowls and place spoonfuls of the mango and lime mixture into the center of each.

 Mango and Coconut Rice Pudding

· Heat through 2 x 400 g (13 oz) cans rice pudding with ½ mango, stoned, peeled and roughly chopped, and 3 tablespoons lightly toasted desiccated coconut. Serve in large ramekins sprinkled with extra toasted desiccated coconut.

 Coconut Rice with Caramelized Banana Place ½ cup Arborio risotto rice in a heavy saucepan with ⅓ cup superfine sugar, 1¼ cups milk and 1¾ cups canned coconut milk. Bring to a boil, then reduce the heat and simmer for 20 minutes until the rice has swelled and thickened. Meanwhile, cut 4 firm bananas in half lengthwise and sprinkle with 4 tablespoons light brown sugar and 1 teaspoon ground cinnamon. Heat a nonstick skillet over high heat and cook the bananas for 2 minutes on each side or until the sugar has caramelized. Spoon the cooked rice onto serving plates and top with the banana slices.

Griddled Madeira Cake with Plum and Berry Compote

Serves 4

2 tablespoons unsalted butter

2 plums, pitted and cut into chunks

1¼ cups fresh strawberries, hulled and halved

¼ cup superfine sugar

½ teaspoon ground cinnamon

2 tablespoons water

1 cup fresh raspberries

4 thick slices of Madeira cake

2 tablespoons confectioners' sugar

- Melt the butter in a heavy saucepan and cook the plums over medium heat, stirring occasionally, for 2 minutes. Add the strawberries, superfine sugar, cinnamon, and measurement water and cook, stirring occasionally, for 2 minutes until the fruit is tender. Stir in the raspberries.

- Meanwhile, heat a griddle pan over high heat. Dredge the cake slices on one side with half the confectioners' sugar and cook, sugar-side down, for 1 minute until warm and scorched in lines, then dredge the other side with the remaining confectioners' sugar and cook on that side for 1 minute.

- Serve the cake slices with the warm compote spooned over.

2 **Plum, Berry, and Madeira Cake Trifles** Melt 2 tablespoons butter in a heavy saucepan and cook 2 plums, pitted and cut into chunks, over medium heat, stirring occasionally, for 2 minutes. Add 1 cup hulled and halved strawberries, ¼ cup superfine sugar, ½ teaspoon ground cinnamon, and 1 tablespoon water and cook, stirring occasionally, for an additional 2 minutes until the plums are tender. Allow to cool for 5 minutes, then spoon the compote into the base of a glass bowl and top with 4 slices of Madeira cake, cut into chunks. Drizzle the cake with 2 tablespoons cream sherry, then pour over 1¾ cups good-quality ready-made fresh custard. Top with spoonfuls of sour cream. Decorate with fresh strawberry quarters.

3 **Plum Compote, Marzipan, and Madeira Pudding** Melt 2 tablespoons butter in a heavy saucepan and cook 6 plums, pitted and cut into chunks, over medium heat, stirring occasionally, for 2 minutes. Add ¼ cup superfine sugar, ½ teaspoon ground cinnamon, and 1 tablespoon water and cook, stirring occasionally, for an additional 2 minutes until the plums are tender. Place in the bottom of a large, shallow gratin dish. Cover with 4 thick slices of Madeira cake, then top with 6 oz grated marzipan. Place in the top of a preheated oven, 375°F, for 15 minutes until the marzipan is browned in places.

Treacle Sponge Microwave Puddings

Serves 4

7 tablepoons butter, softened, plus extra for greasing
½ cup light brown sugar
¾ cup self-rising flour
1 teaspoon apple-pie spice
1 egg, beaten
4 tablespoons corn syrup
custard, to serve

- Lightly grease 4 x ⅔ cup ramekins and line the bases with parchment paper. Beat the butter with the sugar in a bowl until pale and fluffy, then sift in the flour and spice and add the egg. Beat together until well mixed.

- Divide the mixture between the prepared ramekins. Cover each with a disk of parchment paper and cook together in a microwave oven on high for 2–2½ minutes, then allow the sponges to rest for 3–4 minutes to finish cooking.

- Turn each pudding out onto a serving plate and drizzle each with 1 tablespoon of the corn syrup while still warm. Serve with custard.

 Warm Treacle Madeira Cake

Cut 1 store-bought Madeira cake into chunks and place in the base of an ovenproof dish. Place 5 tablespoons corn syrup in a saucepan with 2 tablespoons butter and 2 tablespoons light brown sugar. Heat gently, stirring constantly, for 2 minutes until the syrup is warm and well blended with the butter. Pour over the cake cubes and heat in a microwave oven on high for 1 minute. Serve warm with scoops of ice cream.

 Baked Treacle Sponge

Grease a 4 cup shallow baking dish and spoon in 6 tablespoons corn syrup. In a food processor, whiz together 8 tablespoons each softened butter and superfine sugar, 2 beaten eggs, and 1 teaspoon vanilla extract. Add ¾ cup self-rising flour and pulse until just mixed. Scrape into the baking dish and place in a preheated oven, 350°F, for 25 minutes until golden. Serve with hot store-bought ready-made custard.

3 Chocolate Puddle Pudding

Serves 4

5 tablespoons unsalted butter,
  softened
⅓ cup light brown sugar
3 eggs
½ cup self-rising flour
3 tablespoons unsweetened
  cocoa powder
½ teaspoon baking powder
confectioners' sugar, for dusting
ice cream or cream, to serve

For the sauce

2 tablespoons unsweetened
  cocoa powder
¼ cup light brown sugar
1 cup boiling water

- Grease a 2½ cup gratin dish with a little of the butter. Place the remaining butter, brown sugar, and eggs in a large bowl and sift in the flour, cocoa, and baking powder. Beat together until smooth. Spoon the mixture into the prepared dish and spread the top level.

- For the sauce, place the cocoa and sugar in a bowl and mix in a little of the measurement water to make a smooth paste, then add the remaining water, a little at a time, and mix until smooth.

- Pour the sauce over the pudding mixture and place in a preheated oven, 400°F, for 15 minutes or until the sauce has sunk to the bottom of the dish and the pudding is well risen. Dust with confectioners' sugar and serve with ice cream or cream.

 Chocolate Sponges with Hot Chocolate Sauce Heat 4 store-bought chocolate sponge cakes or muffins in a microwave for 1 minute until warmed through. Meanwhile, mix 1 teaspoon finely grated orange zest into ½ cup clotted cream. Make the chocolate sauce as above. Serve the warm cakes or muffins covered with the hot sauce and topped with a spoonful of the orange cream.

 Chocolate Pancakes with Hot Chocolate Sauce In a food processor, whizz together ¾ cup all-purpose flour, 1 tablespoon unsweetened cocoa powder, 1 egg, and ¾ cup milk until smooth. Heat a little vegetable oil in a nonstick skillet and cook the pancakes in batches, using 6 tablespoons batter at a time, over medium-high heat for 1–2 minutes. Flip and cook on the other side. Remove and keep warm. Make the chocolate sauce as above. Serve the pancakes drizzled with the hot sauce, dusted with confectioners' sugar and with ice cream on the side.

FAM-DESS-DAC

30 Caramel Pear Tarte Tatin

Serves 4–6

butter, for greasing

2 x 13 oz cans pears in
fruit juice, drained

5 tablespoons dulce de leche

12 oz ready-made sweet
shortcrust pastry, defrosted if
frozen

all-purpose flour, for dusting

ice cream or cream, to serve

- Line the base of a 9 inch removable-bottomed cake pan with parchment paper and grease.

- Place the pears and dulce de leche in a saucepan and heat over gentle heat for 1–2 minutes, stirring occasionally, until the pears are well coated in the sauce. Arrange the pears in the base of the prepared pan in a single layer.

- Roll out the pastry on a lightly floured work surface to a circle slightly larger than the pan and place over the pears, folding any surplus up the side of the pan.

- Place in a preheated oven, 425°F, for 20 minutes until the pastry is golden and cooked. Run a knife around the edge of the tart and turn out onto a serving plate. Serve cut into wedges with ice cream or cream.

 Pan-Fried Caramelized Pears

Melt 2 tablespoons butter in a large, heavy skillet. Take 2 x 13 oz cans pears in fruit juice, drain and quarter the pears, and place in a bowl. Coat the pears in 5 tablespoons dulce de leche, then fry until the sauce is bubbling and the pears are softened. Serve with scoops of ice cream, drizzled with caramel or toffee sauce.

 Individual Caramel Pear Tarts

Cut out 4 x 4 inch circles, using a small dish or saucer as a guide, from 12 oz shortcrust pastry and place on a baking sheet. Prick all over with a fork, then place in a preheated oven, 400°F, for 10 minutes until golden. Meanwhile, drain a 13 oz can pears in fruit juice and roughly chop or slice. Melt 2 tablespoons butter in a saucepan and cook the pears over medium-high heat, stirring frequently, for 2 minutes, then sprinkle over 3 tablespoons dark brown sugar and cook, tossing, for another minute. Add 2 tablespoons heavy cream and stir well to make a caramel sauce. Spoon the caramel pears over the pastry disks on serving plates and serve with ice cream, if desired.

10 Scone, Strawberry, and Clotted Cream Trifles

Serves 4

1¼ cups fresh strawberries, hulled and quartered, plus 2 extra, halved, to decorate
4 tablespoons strawberry jam
4 tablespoons clotted cream
2 store-bought plain scones, halved

- Place the strawberries in a bowl and mix with the strawberry jam. Divide half the strawberries between the bases of 4 serving glasses and top each with a spoonful of the cream and then a scone half.

- Spoon over the remaining strawberries, then decorate each trifle with a strawberry half.

20 Scone and Berry Boozy Trifle

Place 1¾ cups fresh hulled strawberries, 1 cup fresh raspberries and 4 tablespoons strawberry or raspberry preserves in a bowl. Mix well, then transfer to a trifle bowl. Roughly chop 4 store-bought plain scones and sprinkle over the top, then drizzle with 6 tablespoons dry sherry. Pour over 2½ cups chilled store-bought ready-made vanilla custard and then spoon over 1¾ cups sour cream. Decorate with halved strawberries.

30 Mixed Berry Compote and

Scone Bake Place 3 cups frozen mixed summer berries in a saucepan with ⅔ cups superfine sugar and 4 tablespoons dry sherry or water. Bring to a boil, then pour into a large, shallow gratin dish. Halve 4 plain scones and arrange, cut-side down, over the compote. Sprinkle with 5 tablespoons Demerara sugar mixed with ½ teaspoon ground cinnamon. Place in a preheated oven, 375°F, for 15 minutes. Serve with custard.

20 Speedy Apple Crumble-Style Desserts

Serves 4

2 tablespoons unsalted butter

2 large cooking apples, peeled, cored, and cut into chunks

4 tablespoons dark brown sugar

4 tablespoons heavy cream

8 tablespoons granola crunchy oat cereal

2 tablespoons toasted slivered almonds

clotted cream, to serve (optional)

- Melt the butter in a heavy skillet and cook the apple chunks over medium heat, stirring occasionally, for 5–6 minutes until tender and browned.

- Add the sugar and cook, stirring, for 1 minute. Add the cream and cook, stirring, for 1 minute more until the sauce is caramel colored and the apples are tender yet still retaining their shape.

- Divide the apple mixture between 4 warmed serving bowls. Mix the oat cereal with the almonds and spoon over the top of the hot apple mixture. Serve with a spoonful of clotted cream on top, if desired.

10 Apple and Raspberry Broiled Crumbles

Mix a 13 oz can or jar prepared apples or apple pie filling with ¾ cup fresh raspberries and divide between 4 individual ramekins. Top with 8 tablespoons granola crunch cereal mixed with 2 tablespoons ground almonds. Dot with butter and cook under a preheated medium broiler for 2 minutes until warm. Serve with vanilla ice cream.

30 Oaty Summer Fruit Crumble

Place 1 lb frozen mixed summer fruits in a baking dish and sprinkle with 4 tablespoons superfine sugar. Melt 7 tablespoons butter and 4 tablespoons corn syrup in a saucepan and stir in 1½ cups rolled oats and 3 tablespoons ground almonds. Spread the mixture over the fruit and place in a preheated oven, 350°F, for 25 minutes until golden. Serve with good-quality vanilla ice cream.

Meringue-Topped Tangy Lemon Cups

Serves 4

finely grated zest and juice
   of 2 lemons
¾ cup superfine sugar
2 tablespoons cornstarch
1 egg yolk
2 egg whites
1 teaspoon light brown sugar

- Place the lemon zest and juice in a small saucepan with half the superfine sugar and ⅔ cups water. Bring to a boil. Meanwhile, blend 3 tablespoons water into the cornstarch in a heatproof bowl, pour over the hot liquid, stirring constantly, and mix well until thickened. Stir in the egg yolk. Return to the pan and cook, stirring constantly, for 1 minute until thickened. Divide between 4 individual ramekins or gratin dishes.

- Whisk the egg whites in a grease-free bowl until stiff. Add 1 tablespoon of the remaining superfine sugar at a time, whisking well between each addition, until the meringue is smooth and glossy.

- Spoon the meringue mixture over the lemon cups and sprinkle with the brown sugar. Place the dishes on a baking sheet and cook under a preheated high broiler for 1–2 minutes until the tops are lightly golden and have firmed a little. Serve warm.

Tangy Lemon Eton Mess

Break 8 store-bought meringue nests into small chunks and place in a bowl. Whip 1¼ cups heavy cream in a separate bowl until thick and mix into the meringue, followed by 1 cup hulled and halved strawberries and 1 teaspoon finely grated lemon zest. Serve in individual glass bowls decorated with mint sprigs.

Tangy Lemon Curd Puddings

In a food processor, whiz together 9 tablespoons each softened butter, ⅔ cup superfine sugar, and 1 cup self-rising flour, 2 beaten eggs, and the finely grated zest of 1 lemon until well blended. Drop 1 tablespoon store-bought lemon curd into the base of 4 individual greased ramekins. Spoon the sponge batter on top, cover with plastic wrap and cook in a microwave oven individually on high for 1½ minutes until risen and cooked through. Allow to rest for 1 minute before serving with vanilla ice cream.

1 Caramel Bananas

Serves 4

2 tablespoons butter
¼ cup light brown sugar
4 bananas, peeled
8 tablespoons heavy cream
vanilla ice cream, to serve

- Melt the butter in a large, heavy skillet, add the sugar, and heat gently until the sugar has dissolved and the butter is foaming.

- Cut the bananas in half lengthwise, then cut each half in half again widthwise. Add to the pan and cook over medium heat, stirring and turning gently once or twice, for 3–4 minutes until softened. Remove with a spatula and divide between 4 warmed serving bowls.

- Add the cream to the pan and stir well with a wooden spoon. Spoon the sauce over the bananas and serve with scoops of vanilla ice cream.

2 Rum and Raisin Banana Pancakes

Make up a 5 oz package pancake mix according to the package instructions. Melt 2 tablespoons butter in a large, heavy skillet, add ¼ cup light brown sugar and heat gently until the sugar has dissolved and the butter is foaming. Cut 4 peeled bananas in half lengthwise, then each half in half again widthwise. Add to the pan and cook over medium heat, stirring and turning gently once or twice, for 2–3 minutes. Add 4 tablespoons raisins and cook for 1 minute more, then add 2 tablespoons dark rum and set alight. Remove from the heat and allow the flames to die down. Heat a lightly greased 9 inch nonstick skillet and cook the batter in 4 batches over medium-high heat for 30 seconds–1 minute on each side until golden. Fill the pancakes with the bananas and serve warm, with ice cream, if desired.

3 Baked Bananas with Chocolate and Honey

Lay 4 unpeeled ripe bananas in a roasting pan and place in a preheated oven, 400°F, for 20 minutes until blackened and very soft. Remove from the oven, make a slit down the skin of each, and drizzle with honey. Sprinkle with 2 oz roughly chopped bittersweet chocolate and serve with spoonfuls of sour cream or ice cream.

 # Quick Tiramisu with Strawberries

Serves 4–6

⅔ cup strong coffee, cooled
⅓ cup light brown sugar
4 tablespoons coffee liqueur
4 oz ladyfingers, halved
1¼ cups store-bought ready-made fresh custard
1 cup mascarpone cheese
1 teaspoon vanilla extract
4 oz bittersweet chocolate, roughly chopped
¾ cup fresh strawberries, hulled and thinly sliced
unsweetened cocoa powder, for dusting

- Place the coffee, sugar, and liqueur in a large bowl. Add the lady fingers and gently toss to soak in the mixture, then transfer to a shallow serving dish, spooning over any excess liquid.

- Beat the custard with the mascarpone and vanilla extract in a separate bowl, then spoon half over the soaked ladyfingers and spread evenly. Sprinkle half the chocolate over the top followed by the strawberries.

- Spoon the remaining mascarpone mixture over the strawberries and spread evenly. Sprinkle with the remaining chocolate and dust with cocoa. Chill until ready to serve.

 ### Irish Cream Liqueur Tiramisu

Press 8 halved ladyfingers into 4 glass serving dishes. Pour over enough cold coffee to soak the sponges. Sprinkle 1 tablespoon Irish cream liqueur over each dish, then top each with 1 scoop Irish cream liqueur ice cream, 1 tablespoon softly whipped cream, and a sprinkling of grated bittersweet chocolate. Serve immediately.

 ### Tiramisu-style Cheesecake

Place 7 oz amaretti cookies in a plastic bag and bash with a rolling pin to form fine crumbs. Mix with 3½ tablespoons melted butter and press into a 7 inch removable-bottomed cake pan. Refrigerate for a few minutes. Dissolve 1 tablespoon instant coffee in 4 tablespoons hot water and 2 tablespoons brandy in a large bowl. Briefly dip 10 ladyfingers in the mixture and set aside. Beat 2 cups mascarpone cheese with 5 tablespoons confectioners' sugar and spread half over the chilled cookie base. Lay the ladyfingers on top and top with the remaining mascarpone mixture. Chill until required and dust with unsweetened cocoa powder before serving. Serve with fresh summer berries, if desired.

Index

Page references in *italics* indicate
photographs

Acknowledgments

Recipes by Emma Jane Frost
Executive Editor Eleanor Maxfield
Senior Editor Sybella Stephens
Copy Editor Jo Richardson
Art Direction Mark Kan
Design www.gradedesign.com
Photographer Stephen Conroy
Home Economist Emma Jane Frost
Prop Stylist Isabel De Cordova
Production Peter Hunt